MW01534594

OOPS

we lost our values

JOHN W. CAMPBELL

OOPS

we lost our values

A Discussion of the Erosion of
Morality and Ethics in The United States

TATE PUBLISHING & *Enterprises*

TATE PUBLISHING
& Enterprises

OOPS, We Lost Our Values
Copyright © 2006 by John W. Campbell. All rights reserved.
This title is also available as a Tate Out Loud audio product.
Visit www.tatepublishing.com for more information.

No part of this publication may be reproduced, stored in a retrieval system or transmitted in any way by any means, electronic, mechanical, photocopy, recording or otherwise without the prior permission of the author except as provided by USA copyright law.

The opinions expressed by the author are not necessarily those of Tate Publishing, LLC.

Book design copyright © 2006 by Tate Publishing, LLC. All rights reserved.
Cover design by Janae Glass
Interior design by Jennifer Redden

Published in the United States of America

ISBN: 1-5988670-0-8
06.11.14

For my parents,
John and Martha Campbell.
Thanks for teaching values by example.

Table of Contents

Preface

Thirty thousand was the number. This number was plastered on the front page of the *USA Today* news paper this morning as the number of Iraqis killed since the beginning of the present conflict. The number was espoused by President Bush during an open question period after a speech he gave about the Iraq conflict. Bush says that 30,000 Iraqi people have been killed. I was appalled but expected it as Fox News reported at the close of the speech and question period that the Associated Press had sent this statement out over their wire to all who would print it. The most important item in the article was the answer to one question about the number of Iraqi civilians killed. I say this because when I took some journalism classes years ago, I was taught to put the most important item in the headline, and then comes the next most important item and so on until the least important item is listed at the last of the article.

News journalism has changed, and mostly for the worst since it seems that making money or selling papers is almost as important as the political bias that is rampant in the reporting. I did not hear the speech, but I did hear most of the question and answer period. The "30,000" number was in answer to a question by a reporter. It seems to me that the number 30,000 turns out to be the number that is given most often by the media and is not news. It became a headline when the President reiterated the same number. The speech was mentioned in the article but I read very little of it. After the headline it was difficult to imagine that the speech would be described in the paper as it was given by the president.

It may seem that I am conservative in my political thinking and this is partially correct. But I should caution you that my conservatism is liberal at times.

I grew up in central New York State during the 40's and 50's, and a large majority of the voters were registered Republican. I now live in northern West Virginia, and the majority of voters are registered Democrats. "So what?" you ask. Well, the Republicans in central New York are much more liberal than the Democrats in northern West Virginia, so when I say I lean to the conservative side, some of my Democratic friends are more conservative than me. Now what does all of this have to do with the *USA Today's* article about the Presidential speech? Before I am a Republican or conservative, I am a patriot and am for the United States of America, and I am against anything that tends or tries to disrespect this country or the political offices that make it function. I did not say that I agree with everything the office holders do or say, but I will not demean them by misquoting or espousing fiction about them.

"Bush puts deaths of Iraqis at 30,000" was the headline printed in the *USA TODAY* on December 13, 2005. The article by Oren Dorell was not fiction but was not the news that should have been reported as to what the President had said about the war. What should have been reported was answers to the following questions: Are we winning? Are things getting better? When are the troops coming home? These questions had been answered as opinions by the president's opposition, but the real news was the president's assessment of the war. The newspaper's first and foremost purpose seemed to be to demean the president rather than tell us the real news.

If you are reading this, you should know that at this point in writing this book, there is no expectations of publishing anything. Since I am retired, I have time to read newspapers and listen to television news and aggravation sets in due to faulty or misleading reporting. To vent my feelings, I sit down at my computer and start writing. It is amazing how much better I feel after writing and reading my thoughts on the problem subject. Today it was the *USA TODAY,* and tomorrow it may be something else, but the reporting of news has become sleazy in the past few years at best and is so unbelievable now that it takes very little to stir me up enough to sit and write.

Each morning I have coffee at a local shop with a few others, some of which are retired. The main topic each day is sports, with the local university taking top billing. Politics are very seldom discussed because there are a couple of Republicans like me, and the rest are Democrats. One word such as *Bush* and we are off and running, with the argument dissolving very quickly to whomever can become the loudest or talk the fastest. There is no room for discussion of right and wrong or whether or not we will win the Iraq War, but the democrats dislike Bush and anything he does and the republicans support him. It is disheartening to me because these people are nice people and have raised very nice families. Their values are high, and they are patriots every day.

Why the tough talk about our president, then? First, I call these people Santa Claus politicians, or those people that were taught by their parents that a certain political party was the only one to be a member of just as they learned about Santa Claus. This political belief never went away as Santa did when they learned the truth about him. Somehow this belief in a political party stuck to them and was never questioned or studied as to philosophy or beginnings. The belief is so strong that it has become more of a religion than politics, and nothing seems to change or alter this belief. People like this deny the things that their party stands up for when it goes against their values, such as abortion and gay rights (which they do not promote), and try to make it as an attack from the opposing party. Why is this important? When the news that is given to us each day through the various outlets is biased and misstated, people that have political beliefs such as mentioned forget the needs of the country as a whole and resort to opposing everything that the other party is doing, whether it is good or bad.

The most troublesome thing for me is the idea that if we lost the Iraq War, it would be bad for Bush, and this is being expressed daily by the media and building hatred in the minds of those that oppose him. Our country losing another war to many is just another day in history, but to me it is a disaster. To think that we as a country can send our young men and women into battle and then just give up the conflict in which they have been engaged is to tell them they do not matter. Since World War II, we have been involved in police actions and undeclared wars that we were winning when it was decided to stop and go home. Korea, Viet Nam and the first Gulf war were examples of not finishing the war that was started. Can you imagine what would happen to a fan base if a college basketball team decided at half time that it was not worth the effort and quit the contest? This is probably not a very good example because the players are not getting killed as soldiers are, but to start a fight or contest and not try to finish it in anything but war is unthinkable for most of us. Our media has joined the opposition to the party in power and has advanced losing the war by just quitting and bringing our troops home. We hear it night after night as TV news reporters interview politician after politician to tell us this message.

A couple of week ago, Senator Lieberman made a statement to the effect that the war in Iraq was going quite well and that the president's plan was working. There was progress being made, and it was possible to win this conflict as planned. This statement was in direct opposition to the Senator's party leaders that were calling for withdrawal and basically the idea that we cannot win. I heard this statement on one news channel but did not hear it on the evening network news. I could not find any mention in our daily paper, and the statement seemed to be buried with the rest of the good news about Iraq. Apparently, the Senator's words did not adhere to the bias of these other news sources, so they did not think it news.

Why are America's news organizations interested in our country losing a war? I cannot understand this philosophy and know it has nothing to do with the reporting of world or national news to the American people. Could it be that political power has become so great in the United States of America that, in order to unseat a political party or to embarrass a president or prove that the party in power is not capable of their offices, it is worth losing a war? Could it be that political offices are so dear as to throw values, morals and patriotism out the window to win election to them? We all know that part of this is true and has been for a long time.

It has been part of our cultural heritage, from the Tories of the Revolution working for the English to the new Constitutional government not willing to finance the War of 1812. We saw it again with the purchasing of men to be drafted in the Civil War by people that did not want to fight and the Jane Fondas and draft dodgers of the Vietnam era. Freedom to all is what we allow in this country, and part of that is the right to disagree with the government. Disagreement and being a traitor are two different things; although to wish our country to lose a war is as close to being traitorous as possible without being prosecuted. The history of this activity in the United States started before the states were united and I guess will continue as long as we can continue to guarantee freedom of speech and freedom of the press. The viciousness of the attacks seems to be increasing, and almost nothing is barred, including senators calling each other derogatory names in their chambers.

My local newspaper is not much different. Almost every day there is a column on the front page with the number of armed forces killed during the Iraq conflict and then the number since the armed conflict ended. Most often, with some exceptions, any positive news inside the paper is hidden on another page. Today there was a front page article about the Iraqi elections opposite the listing of the number killed. The need to put the articles that are sensational on the front page often place the real news hidden in the back pages. I do not understand because none of these newspaper copies are sold by someone standing on the street yelling out the headlines. I have asked to have the number of highway deaths in our area placed on the front page in the same way to raise awareness of highway safety. Sorry, it is not news, and no one cares about that. News that is reported to us each day is rarely the news that we should be hearing, but it is that which will sell advertising and papers or garner radio and TV listeners. We are bombarded with political bias and prejudice every day to attempt to sell us on a particular point of view.

Values

Webster's II New College Dictionary defines "value" as a "return for goods, monetary or material worth" or a "principal, standard or quality regarded as worthwhile." We use this word for a lot of different things, but the greatest of the definitions is the idea of how much the ethics and morals of a society are worth. Our values are measured by how we treat each other and the quality of our civility. I had not thought much lately about values as something that holds societies together until I enrolled my granddaughter into a private school. The admission's officer told us that, along with providing a good education, they would teach values and responsibility. Talk about two powerful words that can stir emotions and controversy. These two seem to have drifted away from our culture somewhat.

Many of the values that we have are held in place by law and statute. Protection of minors, penalties for stealing someone else's property and laws against harming another human being are some of the ways that societies ensure a value system. Since we are a free society, many of the values that we claim to possess, such as courtesy, honesty, integrity, responsibility and respect of others, are held in place by each of us. These values are the glue that binds us as people into a civilized society.

Recently a great American died. Rosa Parks fueled the movement to free the slaves one more time. Think about it; after fighting a civil war that killed over 600,000 to free a people that had darker skins than others, a woman had to sit on a bus and defy the law to demand respect as a human being. She did not ask for anything else—just respect as a human being. A value that we take for granted until it is denied had to be wrenched out of a troubled society that said some human beings were worth more than others. The equality of men as expressed by Jefferson was not believed to be true, and the foundation of our great country had started to crumble. Rosa Parks stopped that crumbling by a simple act of asking for respect as a human being. For this, she went to jail. I guess that respect is quite valuable to some.

The values that we have as children seem to change as we grow and become more like the society in which we live. As a young child, I was raised with a great amount of idealism and a value system that had me believing that anything I did that was bad could be seen by God and the rest of the world. Being bad was calling somebody a name, stealing a cookie, disobeying my parents or teachers and talking when in the company of adults. These were the start of a value system that my parents had decided I needed to let me grow into a good and honest young man. If you remember growing up, maybe you can relate to this type of training, but you might also remember that as you grew older, those restrictions were gradually removed. Growing up was nothing more than doing the things that were prohibited when we were younger. At twelve years, I was allowed to drink coffee, and at thirteen and in the seventh grade, I could enter discussions at the dining table. At eighteen, it was alright for me to smoke and drink beer. Our society has placed age plateaus to be reached for children to start to do so-called adult things. I never understood why many of those things were bad at one age and right at another, but then I guess being an adult meant that sinning and doing bad things were accepted. As I grew, my values changed. Of course when I became a father, the value system was reinstated for my children. Today I look back and am grateful that I had parents that instilled a value system in me and wonder what would have happened if everyone had the same amount of love, encouragement and training. It is not going to happen, and many of the things that were part of my growing up have been reduced to Puritanism and old fashioned. The values that have given me a sense of life, such as respect and responsibility, have been eroded to "get yours first." Just as the news media have become income centers and political action groups, we see values of corporate responsibility give in to greed, and the idea of being a good citizen is beyond us in the work place. The Ten Commandments have become a religious symbol instead of a set of laws on which you can build a civilized society. The Golden Rule has become, "Do it to you before you can do it to me." This glue that is so important is getting thinner and thinner, and some day it will not hold our society in place, as other societies have been destroyed by the same erosion of values.

Education

Education starts when we are born and ends when we die. After instinctively finding the nipple that will deliver milk, we have to rely on someone teaching us just about everything else necessary to live this life. We are taught to use a spoon, and maybe we learn to walk by ourselves, but a little help gets us going quicker. Somewhere we enter a formal educational program called school. It may be nursery school or kindergarten and then the first grade. For the next twelve years, we are exposed to writing, reading and arithmetic, plus history, philosophy, science and hopefully driver's education. To accomplish this, we spend about six to eight hours five days a week with a professional teacher. This teacher has completed college courses that have been deemed necessary to train him or her to teach. Now the teaching philosophers enter in and start to tell us the best way to pound information into our young brains. Small classrooms, open classrooms, books, computers, homework or no homework and so on. Whatever the philosophy, teaching children is hard work and expensive, and of course we as human beings like to make hard work easier and high costs cheaper.

When I entered the first grade (Kindergarten was not offered yet), I sat in a room with about thirty children. Some were with me in the first grade, but others were in the second grade and the rest in the third grade. Three grades in the same room with one teacher. You might ask how that is possible if you have never experienced this type of schoolroom, but we thought it was an improvement over six grades being in the same room. By the time I finished the third grade, I had heard the lessons for that grade three times. I could read and write both in print mode and cursive well enough that anyone could read it. I had received a grade on my penmanship for three years in a row, and at nine years old, I realized that my handwriting told all that would read it what kind of person I was.

You may wonder why this is important to me, but let me relate another story. Years later I worked as a plant manager, and from time to time I had to hire new people, some of which were college graduates. After doing this for a few years, I made one of the requirements of getting a job being able to read the job application. I resorted to what I had learned in the third grade about my character being read in my handwriting. If after a high school or college education a person had yet to learn to write legibly, they probably had not learned much else, either. Education had taken a turn for the worse, and I did not know why. Young people could not read and write and had to get their information from pictures and through their ears. How could a young man or woman be graduated from a high school and not know how to read or write? Remember, hard work and expensive. Those that could not or would not learn at the rate of a high school education in twelve years were simply being pushed along and out the door with a diploma. I was receiving them in the work force, and they could not understand why I would not continue to push them along with the same paycheck as the ones that had actually received an education. The school had deceived them into believing that if they did not want to work as hard or do their homework, they could still receive everything at no extra cost.

Values were not being taught. Responsibility and integrity were dispensed with, and the idea that everyone had to compete in the work place was not presented as a reason to get a good education. Remedial education did not push a little harder to return you to your class level; it simply became the vehicle to get rid of you at graduation. Those who went to fill out a job applications found that learning to read and write was important after all. Their qualifications put them at the bottom of the heap, and they entered adult life behind the curve. No work in school meant that they were going to work very hard for the rest of their lives. They wondered where they went wrong. They didn't; their school system did. Their education was going to be too difficult and too expensive, so why not just throw away those of you that for some reason did not like school or had to study a little harder.

In case you are thinking that I am discriminating against the lower IQ's, please read on. Many of the most successful people, like our president and Senator Kerry, had college accumulative averages in the C plus to B plus range. The most successful people will tell you that getting As was nice, but the hard work necessary to get those Bs and Cs is what made them successful. The work ethic they learned from having to study a little harder carried over into their careers. Our schools are throwing away the people that have the most potential as adults by not pushing and teaching and demonstrating the value system needed to be successful.

We have enlarged our schools to institutions so large that children have become numbers, and many have resorted to some very violent behavior to get someone's attention. It is known that the local school is the best place in which children are able to learn. Being small enough to allow each child to be a real part of the school society and feel included seems to work better than giving each child a number. This has become too expensive for many urban areas, so we end up with these huge facilities that prevent any type of individual attention, and societal competition and pressure become the overriding factor in the education process. The slow are pushed along, and the smart get all of the attention while those in the middle are just so many numbers.

It is almost against the law to try to teach any type of value system because it may be thought of as a religious education. God is not allowed in school, and praying for a good grade is frowned upon. Responsibility, integrity, honesty, respect and courtesy are not present, and discipline is not allowed. Students are not responsible for their homework, and the teacher will probably be sued if they try to keep their classroom orderly through discipline.

My sister-in-law tells me that she has had students stand and call her names and refuse to adhere to any classroom protocol. Her action is to send them to the principal, who sends them back for more of the same. Our schools have become a haven for gangs and junk food, and the locker rooms and bathrooms look more like a dog kennel than a place for civilized people to use. Schools actually sell out to the soft drink companies for some money without any sense of responsibility of nutrition for their students. The money is more important. I believe this trend had been reversed, but why did it start in the first place? Values have been compromised for a few pieces of silver. Values have been compromised to avoid facing discipline problems. Values have been compromised because those institutions that teach our teachers have decided that asking a child to take responsibility is cruel, to discipline a child is hurtful and that teaching values is the same as teaching religion. Most of the professors that teach our teachers have never lived in the real world and have never left university life. Their knowledge is so narrow that relating to a troubled youngster is beyond them. Realizing that their sheltered life is not parallel to the center of the city or the middle of the factory floor is beyond comprehension, but they are the experts. Our universities and the professors of education are doing a terrible job, and if they were in private industry their failure would be apparent much more quickly.

What about the cost of education? The one room school that I attended probably did a better job than any of our schools today. We learned, behaved and enjoyed learning. We shared three grades and learned to respect the grades other than ours. We also learned to take responsibility and be a member of a society of young people. I am not advocating that we return to one room schools, but there is a trend in some parts of the country to return to more than one grade sharing a room. Money will never replace elbow grease and homework; recitation, multiplication tables and memorizing cannot be replaced by computers. We give kids computers before they have learned the skills to use them properly. We give them calculators to prevent them from having to memorize math tables. We use television to baby sit them and think they can become educated by watching educational programming.

We have found that students that watch TV a lot have learned through pictures or visual learning. When we read, we have to know the words, recognize how they are used in a sentence and then translate that knowledge to an image in our brain that we can understand and put into our memory. The TV shortens this process and puts the image into our brain without any effort. After a while we find reading and interpreting what we read as hard work and start to have trouble. We read less and less until we have become reading impaired. Next, we stop trying to write because the keyboard will do it for us, and finally we end up illiterate. A friend of mine that teaches remedial reading told me that television has become the largest cause of poor reading and reading difficulties. It is fun to learn through our eyes, and it is easier than reading, but what you can learn is limited and probably will not get you into a college or a job. Easy is not good, and it is the responsibility of teachers and parents to change our education system back to the hard work of learning. Responsibility is a value that we have to put back into education.

The university is not much better. Freedom of thought and speech is limited in many cases to that which the faculty subscribes. My niece wrote a paper for an English assignment, and it was returned to her as being too conservative. What has conservatism got to do with using good English? Her English professor was also teaching liberalism as an adjunct to English. One of the cable news channels reported that a student in the San Francisco area received an F for writing a paper that agreed with the president on the Iraq war. Imagine an educational institution that is supposed to seek free thought and new ideas, but instead has decided that if you do not think as the faculty does, you have not learned anything correctly. The so-called educated elite in our society have become the extremely narrow-minded. The American farmer is much better educated. His education was real and taken from the natural systems that he deals with each day rather than a narrow view of politics or religion.

It has been reported that some of the Ivy League schools

have classes in which fifty percent of the students have straight As. That is impossible, and everyone that has studied a little math knows what a bell curve is. If the subject matter is given properly and at the proper grade level, it is possible for about five percent of the class to receive an A and about five percent to receive an F. The other ninety percent will get Bs, Cs and Ds. If half of the class is getting As, something is wrong, and the subject matter is too easy or there is a lot of cheating. What really is wrong is that money has commanded high grades for more students so the offensively high tuition can be collected. Along with this, a few more dollars can be wrung out of parents for giving their children such an excellent education. You could not possibly charge all of that money and then flunk the kid. The grades have become worthless as a measurement of a student's progress. Pass/fail would be just as appropriate, and you could increase the subject difficulty level back to that before money took over. The elitism and snobbery of the university system has started to look a lot like that which we fought a revolution to get rid of. Titles have returned, but as PhD and SD and "Professor" and "Doctor" and "President." Education has taken a back seat once again for people to try to discriminate against others by looking down their noses. Remember the longest nose belonged to Pinocchio.

College loans guaranteed by the federal government came about as a program to allow more students a chance at higher education. They have done that and more. The "more" is that colleges and universities have been able to throw fiscal responsibility out of the window and just raise and raise their tuition. The government will pay for it, and it has; except that now we have students graduating with loans greater than home mortgages to repay as they enter the work force. Of course many of these loans never get repaid, and once again the taxpayer is left with the cost of exorbitant tuition. Once again the government has stuck its nose into the private sector and made a mess of things. Think about where tuition would be if there were no government guaranteed loans today. Sure, some young people would have to work a little harder as I did, but the cost of their education would be something they could afford.

You may wonder what all of this diatribe is leading to or why I make all of this noise. I suppose I could run for the local school board, but in West Virginia it is political, and you have to become a politician first. This should tell you a little about our problems with education. So let's think about what you may want your children to learn while in school. Of course you want them to be prepared to go to college if possible, and they will be if they wish, but how about some of the other things that life throws at us? Will they be prepared? How about teaching them to make a family budget and how to follow it? How about bringing in a psychologist and a marriage counselor and members of the local clergy to teach your children how to get along with each other or how to look for a mate and what type of person to avoid when dating? How about sex education? Today we start in grade school and tell them about the birds and bees, including homosexuality, but never try to teach the responsibility that goes along with sex.

Back to the old one room school and sex education. Our area was agrarian, as was most of the country at that time. Sex education was learned behind the barn, not with the neighbor girl or boy, but by observing the cow and bull or the ram and ewe. We not only learned about the sex act, we then had to feed and care for the baby animals produced by that act. Responsibility became part of the lesson every time I held the pail of calf food or taught the young animal to drink. It was my job in the summer to wean and feed all of the new calves. Today, sex is taught with the expectation of needing protection from disease and pregnancy instead of teaching it for the reason for its being. "Don't get pregnant" or "Don't get a disease" or "Don't get caught" are the messages rather than, "Take responsibility for your actions, and if you cannot wait for marriage, be ready to care for the results of that action."

I have thought for a long time, or at least since the sixties and the sexual revolution, that if it were mandatory for young people to put up bonds to care for the children they may produce before they engaged in sex, we might be able to close a lot of orphanages.

Most of the sex education is taught in the movies and on television, and the results of the acts are usually portrayed as the same as getting off the carnival ride. Just another form of entertainment as peddled by the pornographer as he enters our homes and invades the minds of our children as part of the art of literature and film. We can do much better than this for our young people and actually help them to enjoy sex within their own family situation more as they age. Hollywood portrays sex much the same as a dog kennel, with the lead male conquering every female he runs into—just what we want our children growing up thinking proper behavior is. Values have been erased from the expected responsibility of sexual encounters, and the way in which we procreate has been reduced to fun and entertainment.

What would be wrong with teaching the child that did not want to go to college how to be a construction worker or truck driver with the skills that help him or her to own their own business some day? Why not introduce the stock market as a way to increase wealth? I learned about investing in this country's businesses at forty years old. It was never taught in high school or college, and I would not have been aware of investing but for an entrepreneur that started the company for which I worked. He suggested that if we believed in our company, we should accept stock options and invest in it. I did, and so did many others working there who now do not have to worry about their retirement. How had I missed this for twenty years and not become part of the investment community other than by having a savings account and life insurance? The education system had failed me and many others, and it is still failing our children today.

An attempt has been made to allow some of our social security taxes to be invested into private securities. This attempt has been brushed aside by many politicians and special interest groups such as the AARP. The AARP with its insurance business is highly invested in the private sector but is against the rest of us enjoying the same returns. For the life of me, I cannot understand why anyone would not want to teach all of America about becoming owners of the businesses that make this country great. Again, political power and bias have precluded the value system, and those that may have been able to raise their retirement incomes have been told to stay where they are. Stay in your place because you probably cannot understand and use the same methods to increase wealth as the elite have. "We did not teach you how to do this in school, and please do not learn anything about it now" is the message.

Wow! What a slam at the values we use to have and use. Do not teach responsibility and honesty, and forget that part of education that would actually help young people compete as they enter the adult world. Start them off with a mortgage and no skills at relationships. Send them into the world with the idea that they should get theirs before somebody else gets it. They can cheat, steal and refuse responsibility until they get caught. Hopefully they will learn enough about life to sustain them before they fall down and the people they are trying to beat run them over.

Education is what keeps us from just becoming another part of the animal kingdom without any idea why we are here or where we are going. A few years ago there was a poll taken about cheating, and the results were that over half of the business students in this country's most prestigious colleges said that they cheated and thought that they would have to cheat when they entered the workforce to compete. They were being taught that values were worth nothing and would only hinder their progress up the ladder of success. The values of honesty and integrity were pushed aside for better grades, and some thought that they had to do the same when they entered the business community. My sister-in-law tells me that her high school students use their cell phones to text message during tests for answers to questions on the test. The cell phones are not allowed but are smuggled into the test for this new way of cheating. We have seen the results of this thinking in the Enrons and Adelphias. All of the sudden, the lack of values led to breaking the law, and a lot of innocent people were hurt. We can do a lot better, and to start, we need to put a value system back into the education system.

I went to the bookstore recently to buy another book of history. I had to ask if they had it and then where to find it. As I approached the counter, I could see some new magazines in front on display. One of them had this grotesque figure of the president's head on a small body inside of a bubble, acting as if he were trapped and trying to get out. The magazine was *Newsweek*. I did a double-take because at first I thought it might have been the old *Mad* magazine that did have pictures such as this on their cover. It was not *Mad* but one of our countries' major news magazines that is published weekly and reaches much of the world. The caption under the picture said, "Bush's World." The news magazine printed its opinion page on the cover. What was really remarkable was the fact that this so-called news magazine had illustrated their bias against the president on their front page. There was no more guessing about whether or not their publication was biased toward a liberal agenda, and the news they printed was suspect. Their new name should be *The Democratic Party Newsweekly Magazine*, therefore ending the subterfuge displayed as a news source that the American can count on.

Well, since I am tilted toward the conservative view, it is expected that I would object to such a violation of trust in news reporting. Wait a minute because I am just as appalled at the same treatment by a conservative news publication. I can make up my own mind about whether or not the news is good or bad and whether or not I am for or against something based on my political beliefs. I cannot make a judgment about news that is faulty when reported and that cannot be trusted due to the built in bias during the printing of it. What is true and what is false and what is left out to satisfy that bias? There are opinion pages that are inserted into newspapers and magazines to allow bias to be pursued by editors and their staff, but that is not usually on the front cover. A magazine that lives on American dollars and is printed to dispense news to all of America and many foreign countries apparently wishes to tell everyone that the American president is living in a bubble and cannot get out. I would expect this kind of propaganda from a country that considers it to be an enemy or in competition with the US but not from a publication that makes its living on the support of the American people. We deserve much better.

In November 2004, over fifty-one percent of the Americans that voted chose George Bush to be president. If you voted for him, you also voted for his agenda, but if you voted against him, he is still your president for four years. He represents all of us, and we owe him the respect that he earned by winning the election by a majority of those that voted. I do not agree with a lot of his policies and do agree with others, but to abase him and his office on the front page of an American news magazine demonstrates a lack of respect for the president and the people that voted for him.

I have thought about this cover and the message it sends and cannot determine in any way how it conveys anything but utter hatred. It is beyond my thinking to believe that an educated writer and editor decided to tell the World that they thought of our president in this way.

Corporations

A corporation is an entity created by law to allow individuals to do business as a nonhuman. GM is not human but is run by humans, and if you sue GM, you sue a corporate entity, not a human being; therefore any punishment handed out against GM is in the form of fines or restitution, and it will not or cannot go to jail. Corporations or limited liability partnerships allow the creation of partnerships with others in which no individual partner may be left holding the bag. It works quite well for the most part and allowed us as individuals to become a part of huge businesses by buying stock in them. The pooling of talent and money have made us prosper while building systems, buildings and technology that is way beyond what any individual could accomplish. Some corporations are owned by individuals and others by thousands of stock holders. There are laws that govern corporations and how they may conduct business. Some corporations are non-profit, such as churches and local clubs. There are many types of these, and they are restricted in what they may do or give money to. Of course most corporations are for-profit companies, and their existence was created to make money by selling a service or a product.

You might ask what this has to do with values. Corporations are extensions of humans, and values for the corporations should not be different than those for the people running them. Guess what? It does not work that way today. We saw an increase in energy prices, with gasoline rising over 100 percent after a devastating hurricane. I received word that the heating costs for my home were going to increase by twenty-five or thirty percent this year. We are told that our capitalistic system allows these prices to be market driven and to just pay them. Do you think that if your neighbor owned the gas well and told his customers that he was raising his price by twenty-five percent that nothing would happen? First of all, he would not treat his neighbors that way unless he had experienced something catastrophic. Put your neighbor in charge of the huge energy company from whom you purchase your gas, and now he is not doing anything to you. The corporation is, and that is just business. I mention this because my area is covered with gas wells, and they have not experienced any catastrophic happenings; and those whose property they are on have not been given any great increase in benefits. The gas in the gulf is more expensive, so that means that the gas coming out of our local wells is worth more immediately. For years, gas customers have purchased from this company and provided it with profits, and now these same customers are helpless to resist the enormous rate increase. We do not have a choice because we have one gas line into our homes, and it is connected to the gas company's equipment. We used to call this a monopoly and regulate the business to prevent price gouging, but for some reason monopolies, like the gas company and the power company and the telephone company, can grab their pound of flesh whenever they wish.

A few years ago, as the telephone companies were vying for customers after de-regulation, I signed up with MCI for long distance service. We had to elect one of the companies and then pay a fee to our local company for the use of their lines. MCI had run television ads saying that if we were to sign up with them we could call long distance for ten cents a minute any time of the day. This was about what the others were offering but sounded a little better because of no monthly charge. I received my first bill, which was separate from the local bill, and found that I was paying about fifteen cents a minute instead of the ten I expected. I called MCI customer service and was told that there was an increase in rates just after I had signed with them and that if I would read the small print at the bottom of my agreement, I would find that they reserve the right to raise or lower their rates at any time. I had read this because I have grown very wary of fine print. It is "fine" to prevent us from reading and understanding it. After a few months, I noticed that the MCI bill was getting larger, and I was paying twenty-eight cents per minute for my long distance. I called again and was told that if I wanted to get a cheaper rate I would have to sign up for one of their calling plans. I told them that I thought that was what I had done originally but again was referred to the fine print. This time I had to pay a monthly fee to receive a lower cost per minute on my long distance. Since our long distance calls are very few and short, this did not sound very good, but I had to sign up for something, so let's go. After a few months I checked the long distance bill and found that after adding all of the charges together or the monthly and timed charges, I was paying thirty-four cents a minute. They had gotten me again.

Think about a salesman coming to your door and offering to sell you a new vacuum cleaner for one hundred dollars. When the cleaner is delivered, the price has risen to two hundred dollars, and after a few months the bags for the cleaner have tripled in price. We call this a scam, and the scam artist is run out of town or put into jail or charged with a crime. What the scam artist did not know was that if he had formed a corporation and altered his presentation with some added fine print, the scam would have become good business.

The above example is a corporation that has thrown all values that individuals hold dearly out of the window, and those running the company have decided that since they will not have to face their intended customers, they will let them become victims instead. Their presentation is called marketing, but the salesman using the same technique is called a scam artist. Many of our oldest and greatest corporations have thrown all values out of the window and decided that it is proper and fitting to throw all of the Madison Avenue propaganda and all of the schemes thought to be fraudulent if done by individuals at each of us to increase their profits. It is one against thousands, and we lose every time. Its business, and that makes it okay. Sorry, but when you approach a citizen of this country or any other, there is a responsibility, honesty and integrity that are being purchased with the products and services you are selling. Buyer beware is the call to action now.

During the seventies, the Japanese had started to make inroads into our economy, and a local company in central New York was experiencing a lot of competition from Japanese versions of their products. This company requested a visit from the US state department to discuss this problem and possibly get tariffs on the imported goods. I was told by one of those present in the meeting that the state department representative looked out of the window in the conference room and asked who owned the Jaguar? He then asked who owned the VW and the Austin Healy and the Audi. After hearing the answer to his questions, he said that he did not see any problem with imported products and left.

There was a recession in our economy in the early eighties, and since I had a good job and felt secure with a good salary, I decided to buy a new automobile. I did not need a new car, but the purchase might put someone back to work and therefore do a small part in giving the economy a boost. I had to order the car and then waited nine weeks for its arrival. At delivery I relearned the lesson given by the state department official years earlier. On the edge of the door was a label stating that the new Oldsmobile was made in Canada. My attempt to help an American company and maybe keep someone from losing their job was in vain. It seemed to me that GM had deserted its American company image for the international community. The manufacture and sale of an American automobile to help the economy apparently was not in its plans. This was an American company that had gone global but was the largest company in the world because of the freedom allowed by the American Constitution. The workers that had made this company great were not important, and the American customers did not count. Make money any way possible. Since that time, I have not bought an American automobile because I cannot find one. It has been said that the Japanese Honda and Toyota are more American with parts and labor than any of the recognized American companies. Values thrown out the windows for greed have caused Americans to decide to take profits over any loyalty to their workers and customers. By the way, the people who make the cars are also customers.

Those of us that were around during and after World War II can remember calling the telephone company or the power company and hearing a cheery "Hello. How may I help you?" Today it's "Push one if you are having an emergency," or as the gas company says, "If you are having an emergency or an explosion, push one." The contractor that built my home told me that after many calls to the gas company to start my service, he gave up and drove to their office, which is in another town. As he entered, he saw someone that he knew and asked him if he was "push one" or "push two." The rest of the people in the office erupted into laughter. They were aware of the reduction in customer service and heard about it from their neighbors often. Customer service has become "customer serve yourselves, and take your chances." It saves the company money to not hire a telephone operator, so the robotic answering machine takes over, and we are left with something less than a raving idiot to take care of our problems.

Lately it has become vogue to hire someone in India to answer your call for help and then see if you can understand the conversation. I cannot imagine anyone in India giving a darn about my printer that all of the sudden is causing my computer to dial out to AOL without my input. In fact, when I called they said that I should hang up and call back to see if I could get someone in the US to help me. After about thirty minutes, I did reach someone, but by that time the printer was halfway out of the window. HP is making money, and I am aiding and abetting their lack of values each time I purchase one of their products. Responsibility to honor their warrantees and honesty with their customers has been eroded to the point that I as a customer have become just another profit center and not a human being. This is sad because this is one of the companies that drove the computer generation with its operating system and software components to aid the scientific community instead of the business world. I just bought a new printer for my granddaughter, and the cord to connect it to her computer and an extra ink cartridge caused the price to double. I guess it is just some more of that Madison Avenue marketing to get me to believe that the printer was cheap. I told my granddaughter that she would have to call someone in India if she needed help.

Many of the new corporations are small and have replaced small, single owner businesses. The local lawyer is now a corporation, and probably the biggest change in corporate structure is the local doctor. The general practitioner of old has been replaced by a medical corporation. You do not go to the doctor any more; you go to the clinic, which is a group of doctors practicing various specialties with nurses and an office staff. The old medical practice that was in the doctor's home has been replaced by a new polished stone and glass building that looks like a mini hospital. Oh, the county or city hospital has also become a privately operated corporation. What caused this change is the same thing that has raised the price of medical treatment to levels far above what we can afford. Money, money and more money. When the federal government decided to pay for medical treatment and many of the associated items, it became a mad rush to find a way to cash in on this new pot of gold. We will discuss Medicare later, but for now, back to corporate values.

When a doctor had a practice in his home, many times he worked as a private contractor with no protection from liability other than an insurance policy. He was responsible for all of his equipment, office staff and a nurse if he had one. He operated a business, and he charged accordingly. All of the sudden, the new doctor went to medical school, and tuition went up and up because the new student loans would cover them. When this young doctor left school, internship and residency, he or she was in debt up to their ears, and trying to outfit a new office was going to be difficult. Enter the entrepreneur with an idea. Start a medical corporation and hire the new doctor. The new doctor will be paid a salary with a minimum that will get him here, and then when he brings in a certain level of business, he will get a raise or a bonus. The doctor's office has become a corporation with much more than his personal income to be covered with his fees. The doctor's fee is now covering the cost of the rent, the nurse, the office, the equipment and some profit for the stockholders.

Now we have this new corporation, but another corporation called an insurance company has been paying the bills and is resisting the huge raise in fees. They get together and fix the fees that the insurance will pay as a percentage of the fee or a discounted fee. Guess what? That negotiation is between those entities and is not extended to you or me as individuals. The fees charged to us are payable in full if we have no insurance. The big corporations have got us again. I am still waiting for someone to take a medical corporation to court for price fixing and unfair or discriminatory practices, but so far nothing. Individuals cannot buy enough politicians to change this yet.

If you are in need of medical attention, get ready because you will be blackmailed for unreasonable fees and charges. Pay up or stay sick. Many Americans are the victims of this practice but could afford reasonable charges if they were included in the discounts. Why does a huge insurance company pay fifty dollars for an office call at the doctor's office, and the individual without insurance has to pay over one hundred dollars for the same office call? Values have disappeared from the practice of medicine and been replaced with greed. Making a profit is not enough, but a huge profit is expected; and many who enter the medical field will tell you up front that they are in it for the money. The greater tragedy is that those paying the bills are the taxpayers, and as the government assumes more and more of the medical financial responsibility, the number of ways to get rich quick with the government's money will increase.

Let's go back to the newspaper industry. On December 16, 2005, James Risen wrote an article in *The New York Times* about the president spying on telephone conversations without court orders. Apparently the president has authorized the NSA to listen in on conversations from overseas sources to people in the United States. The people being spied on were known or suspected terrorists. The paper's view was that the president was doing something illegal. It was reported that the paper had learned about this procedure a year before running the story. It was also reported that the paper had checked with the White House and been asked not to run the story due to national security.

You may ask what this has to do with values. The person that leaked the story to the paper was a traitor. He or she aided and abetted the enemy if this was reported to the public. *The New York Times* has not acknowledged this, and further, the editor and reporter would probably go to jail to protect their identity. Okay, protect your sources, but if the paper thought that the president was breaking the law as they indicate in subsequent articles, why wait for one year to do something about it? Why not go to the Justice department or their own lawyers or the closest senator and get an investigation started? It became apparent to me that the article was saved for the most opportune moment to embarrass the president, and it happened that both the Iraqi election was successful and the Patriot Act was up for renewal. The moment was right to stop the president's popularity from climbing any higher, and it was worth forgetting about national security and any responsibility as an American corporation for the sake of a scoop. An American company that makes its money from American people sold their customers down the river for what they thought was glory. Values went out the window.

The press has freedoms in this country that exist in no other country, and we will return to discuss this freedom later.

There are many examples of corporations throwing responsibility and integrity away for profits and doing things that the individuals running the company would not do to their neighbors. Do you believe that your neighbor who may be part of a food company would come to your house and tempt your children with candy, soft drinks and all of the snacks available today? No is the answer, but then why does that same neighbor work at an ad agency or a cereal company or a soft drink company and enter your living room every time your child turns on the TV and try to get them to ask you to buy these items? Selling to children is a complete lack of values, especially if what you are selling will harm them. It is well known that watching too much TV will impair reading skills, but the media outlets do everything possible to keep youngsters in front of the screen. They are taught everything from atheism to homosexuality and told that this is normal. The family values are completely discarded because they do not agree with the valueless opinions of the major networks and producers of the shows being aired.

Many of our corporations have replaced the Fiefdoms and castles of old. The kings, queens and princes have become the corporate CEOs, CFOs and COOs. People that have attained a great amount of power start to believe that they are above the rest of mankind in their worth and value. Many had to dispose of any value system to get to their positions and now feel they are worth millions of dollars in salaries and have earned the right to ride around the World in brand new G-5s. Is this wrong that someone can excel and reach the ultimate position? Absolutely not, but there is a responsibility that goes along with their salaries and airplanes. We have seen what happens when officers of large companies forget about that responsibility. The people that provided the funding for their company and the people that go to work every day to make the products or create the services that bring the company its livelihood are left without all that they have worked for. Many times the officers have been able to retain fortunes at the stockholder's and employee's expense when exposed for their crimes. The values of any company will never be any greater than those expressed and demonstrated by the officers that run the company.

Labor Unions

Labor unions have a long history in America and were started out of necessity. As one studies this history, it turns from the early needs in the sweat shops and coal fields to the large union corporations that represent all workers against many smaller corporations. We have just seen some of the negative aspects of unions as the transit workers in New York City decided to strike a few days before Christmas 2005. After three days they went back to work, facing huge fines and loss of wages for their illegal activity. They picked the busiest time of the year to try to blackmail the city into meeting their demands, but the strike was illegal. Their union leaders had decided that their contract wishes were important enough to break the law, and the members followed along like lost sheep. They tried to paralyze the very entity that pays their salary at the time of the year that will affect many more people than their employers. It was not in the best interest of the workers if they wish to gain any sympathy from the public.

Let's look at what these transit workers have. A bus driver in New York City can make a good salary with retirement benefits including medical insurance starting at fifty-five years old. The medical benefit today costs about four or five hundred dollars per month, or rounded to $6,000.00 per year. If the driver lives to the expected average age of seventy-five, they will have received their retirement with cost of living raises and medical insurance for twenty years. Somewhere around sixty-five to seventy years of age, they will start to receive social security Medicare benefits to supplement the medical insurance. Guess what? The bus driver wants more and would like to retire sooner. Of course, after retirement, the bus driver will get another job with a government agency such as the post office and start to earn another retirement benefit, which will become double dipping.

Have you stayed at a New York City hotel lately? If you have, you have noticed that taxes totaling twenty-five percent of the hotel charges have been added to your bill. You will pay a hefty income tax in the city, and the cost of doing business is extremely expensive. The city has been near collapse from debt, and the increase in taxes has driven many businesses out of the city. What has this to do with bus drivers? First, let's understand that I believe that every person that works at a meaningful job should make enough money to live comfortably with affordable food, clothing, shelter and entertainment. I do not believe that because you wish to make more money than your job is worth you have a right to blackmail a complete city.

Most of our states, cities and local communities have started to have budget shortfalls, and much of it can be traced to the way we have structured the remuneration of the government employees needed to run the systems we expect. After World War II, most communities were served by people that were grossly underpaid. To make up for the low pay, they were given more holidays with pay and increases in benefits, such as earlier retirement plans. In fact, most police departments were run as military units with officers on duty for twenty-four hours a day with monthly passes and then thirty days off per year. I remember when New York State Police went from twenty-four-hour duty to twelve-hour duty. The police officers could leave the barracks each day and go home to their families. Soon it was decided that they should not have to work any longer than anyone else, and the eight-hour day was started with only forty hours per week. The reduction in hours caused the need to increase the force to make up for the hours not covered, but as the hours were reduced, the military style retirement after twenty years at half pay was not changed. Now we have three times as many police officers making the same pay, and they may retire after twenty years at half pay. I am not criticizing the pay of police officers because it usually is still too low, but I am trying to make a point of how labor has changed in a few short years in the government working area.

Those workers with the low pay and good benefits started to unionize and demand higher wages that were equal to those of the private sector. After time, this was accomplished but without the loss of the benefits of early retirement and forever medical insurance coverage. All of the sudden the tax structure could not handle the increased burden, so here comes the sales tax and the city income tax and the hotel tax and so on. Higher pay without fiscal responsibility has become the norm for both unions and government, and we saw it again in the bus strike in New York City. What is a bus driver worth? I cannot answer that question because New York City has priced itself out of my reach, and I will not be taking the bus soon. The hotel maid or the waiter in the restaurant or the office clerk that is without much labor protection does care, and when the bus costs more than they can pay, it will become worthless to them.

Labor unions originated as guilds to represent various labor skills. There was a mason's guild and a stone cutter's guild. These guilds became the organization that sponsored the training of young people just beginning to learn a trade or the apprentice. During the Industrial Revolution, the need for someone or something to aid and help the factory worker spawned the spread of the guild into the labor union. The guild was going to represent all workers with or without a skill. The early factories had turned their workers back into the indentured servitude from which they thought they had escaped. Men and children worked from dawn to dusk daily without a decent wage or any type of benefit. The factory owner was getting wealthy off of their backs.

I can see vestiges of the inhumane treatment of coal miners as I drive around West Virginia. I pass communities that have been abandoned but still stand as shacks that were built for miners when they were paid in company script. These people needed work so badly that they accepted jobs in the mines. The mine owners paid them in script or money minted by the mining company. You could use the script in the company store or pay rent to the company. It was worthless anywhere else. Your were paid a little less than you had to spend to eke out a bare existence, and after a few short months you were trapped without any way to escape. Your family grew up with the increasing debt to the company store and was forced to continue in the same way, with generation after generation becoming indentured servants without any time limit. A song by Tennessee Ernie Ford recorded in the fifties called *Sixteen Tons* describes the life of the coal miner, with the last line saying that "I owe my soul to the company store."

The labor unions arrived, and the organizing effort caused wars in the mine fields. Once organized, the union miners started to cause change for the better. The threat of shutting the mines down forced the mining companies to treat their employees as human beings and pay them accordingly. The United Mine Workers went after better pay, better working conditions, safety programs and benefits that today are as good as any in the industry.

The need for labor to be represented had been demonstrated, and unions spread throughout the country. Somehow the labor movement realized that to be effective, they had to become involved in politics, and this has changed what labor unions are about forever. Unions grew larger and larger but never were considered a monopoly under the Sherman Antitrust Act as were the companies they were negotiating with. One international union represents all of the auto workers in the country and negotiates with each of the companies included in their membership. Why this was never changed, and it has been proposed, is beyond me except that these same unions have become some of the largest contributors to political parties in the country. The lobbying effort that was started to change labor laws changed into a full fledged political movement, with the dues collected from all political persuasions given to one political party. That party has usually been the Democratic Party, with attempts to change the practice by Republicans rebuffed time after time. The other thing that has happened is that the unions that were created to represent labor against large corporations have themselves become large corporations. By starting to offer their members retirement plans and negotiating to take them over from companies, they have become some of the wealthiest corporations in the country. We now see labor unions doing the same things that they used to fight against, and the huge pools of money have caused many to misuse their members' retirement plans and dues.

The need for the individual to be represented by some form of collective bargaining unit has become a way of life for many. The need has been reduced by the passing of laws against discrimination, child labor, minimum wages, health and safety and many more. The political power of the larger unions has turned them into corporations that exist for themselves instead for the wishes and needs of the members that they represent. They were started to inject a moral and ethical treatment of workers by employers and to set a standard of values when using human beings for laborious reasons. The values of responsibility, honesty and equity of pay for like jobs were insisted upon by the early unions. The value of an honest day's work for an honest day's pay was forced into reality.

There is a part of unionism that has performed the opposite of that for which they were formed. In 1956, I got a job at GE in Syracuse after finding out that I did not have enough money to return to college. The job was in a twenty-acre building with a few thousand others on three shifts making television sets. My starting wage was about $2.50 per hour, which happened to be what my mother and father made together. At eighteen years old, I was earning more than my dad, and I only had to work eight hours a day with two paid breaks and a lunch period that was unpaid. I was told that I had a choice as to whether or not I joined the International Union of Electrical Workers. Being young and inexperienced, I felt that I had to join to be accepted, and away I went to start paying my first union dues. After about two months on the job, the steward came to me and said that there was a planned walkout for our shift the next day. After asking why, he told me that some workers were protesting because they felt that they were working in an area that was too warm. The next day came, and I reported to work as did most of the shift. The walkout was a bust, and those that did join in were disciplined. After a year and a half and the second layoff, I decided to return to school. The IUE at GE continued to harass the company for the next few years until it was announced that the TV departments were shutting down. Thousands of people lost their jobs. Thousands of salaries that were way above what most people were making at that time were lost because a labor union had become so powerful that they could insist on throwing away the need for GE to compete with other companies for their share of the market and demand more money and benefits. No one was being treated as the miners in West Virginia had been, nor was there any discrimination or lack of benefits. The union could shut the company down at will, and this type of black-mail became too expensive for the company if they were going to continue to compete for business. The union had forgotten their purpose and did the opposite. It had cost thousands of people their jobs. The values that had been fought for were forgotten and discarded. Responsibility, honesty and integrity were not needed when greed and power took over.

We have seen this scenario happen too often in our country, but the lessons of the past have not kicked in yet. It is still happening. First, the auto industry found that it could not compete with foreign imports. This happened after the auto industry had already moved many of their facilities to Canada to get away from excessive labor trouble. The next industry to be brought down was the steel industry. I drive to Pittsburgh now and visit a new shopping center that used to be a steel mill. It still stands with its rusting towers and furnaces as a monument to the industry that was Pittsburgh a generation ago.

The city has not fully recovered, as it neared a collapse in its ability to finance the city's business and services. The state had to step in and oversee the budget process. Now you might say that all of this could not have happened just because of labor unions and their demands, and you are correct. It took much more, but the lack of values on both sides and the need to get rich quick forced the businesses to take the money and run instead of investing in the future. The retirement packages with the associated lifelong medical benefits have disappeared, and the retirees that thought that they had negotiated a good contract have found themselves heading toward poverty.

We find the airline industry going through the same problem now, with some of them failing and many that have discontinued their retirement plans and medical plans for retirees. The labor unions have made a grave error in judgment that their power of numbers can ask for anything they want and get it. The employer's responsibility has increased from paying a salary for work done to complete financial planning for retirement. We have grown up being told that whomever we work for is supposed to take care of us until death. As one of my former bosses told me, "We don't hire people any more; we adopt them." We want to be taken care of rather than accept the responsibility to take care of ourselves.

This country was founded on the principal of equality, or that we each had the opportunity to make our own way in the world without government influence. We could buy land or start a business or just go to work for someone else. It was never thought that after a day's pay for a day's work the employer owed us any further compensation. We may have received room and board as part of our compensation, but that ended when the job ended. We have taken the rights of the worker to mean much more than ethical treatment and payment in real money.

My son had a job when he was in high school at the local

grocery store. After school he would bag groceries and carry the bags to the customer's car. He received the minimum wage and no benefits as a part time worker. After working for one month, he noticed that his pay was short. It was not a little short, but he had a check for less than half of his usual take home pay. He was informed that he would see this for the next three pays, as his initiation fees for his union membership were due. He had no choice since it was a closed shop. After the initiation fee was paid, he would have dues deducted each month. His minimum wage had become much less than the amount proscribed by law, and it was legal. This young high school lad was joining the growing number of workers that received no union benefits but were used to bankroll the union's treasury.

If you remember the movies about the Cosa Nostra or the Mafia of old, then you will remember the mob forcing businesses to pay for protection or be beaten or driven out of business. My son was being forced to pay tribute to have a job at the lowest level in the store. This practice is at every grocery store in town, and I have never heard of or seen a union spokesman try to do anything against this practice. The very unions that are supposed to represent their members are now doing the very same things that they fought wars in the coal fields to stop. Living off of kids is not something that any organization should be proud of, but it is a reality.

Compare this with the war against Wal-Mart that is being prompted by the union movement. Apparently the unions want more dues from minimum wage workers. They should go back to the grocery stores and make some changes before they increase their lack of values in the department store area.

A few years ago, I read an article in one of the business

magazines that the Empire State Building was constructed in thirteen months. The article pointed out that today it would take three years to complete the same structure. The number of bricks laid in a day and the other skills are regulated by union contracts. That is with unlimited resources and today's modern equipment. It is not all bad because some of the labor laws and restrictions were necessary and have made the construction trades safer and allowed the people working in these trades to make enough to live on.

The labor movement today is still the main vehicle for teaching many of the skills needed and provides many of the benefits of retirement plans and medical insurance that individuals would not have without their unions. Some of these trades are the plumbers, lithographers, electricians, masons and stone cutters. I have a cousin that receives his retirement from the carpenter's union. He told me that without the union to find him work and cover his medical and retirement plans, he would have had to find work elsewhere. These unions are still bringing values to historic professions that may be lost without them. Many of the standards and building codes have been promoted by trade unions and the unions insist on adherence to them. These unions are as needed as the contractors that they provide with skilled workers.

The values of respect, responsibility, honesty, integrity and courtesy are the missions of the labor union that is working for its members while giving the same respect to the employers that provide them with jobs. Our value system has to be a two way street if it is to work.

Medicine

The practice of medicine started as a religious function in many cultures. Some of the African and South American tribal groups still have a Medicine Man to mete out cures and controls of disease and injury. Medicine eventually evolved into one of the studies of philosophy and stayed there for many centuries. The four humors had to be in equilibrium for wellness, and bloodletting was one of the best ways to bring this about. The study of medicine started as apprenticeships and finally became a subject to be taught at the college level. When I visited St. Andrews, Scotland, a couple of years ago, I was told the university at St. Andrews was one of the first to offer a medical degree. When I returned home, my oph-thalmologist said the same thing, as he had studied at St. Andrews University.

The medical practice today has departed any religious affili-ation, and the humors have been left behind to be replaced with science. Philosophy and religion have been replaced by objective laboratory study. Anatomy, physiology, chemistry, physics and psy-chiatry are the subjects of the modern doctor. The apprenticeship is still used but only after extensive study of science. Students learn with on-the-job training given by their professors. Our modern doctor is the most educated and knowledgeable person ever to treat disease or injury. Medical conditions caused by disease and injury are being successfully treated today that were hopeless just a few years ago.

As the practice of medicine became more scientific and started to push the average life span from the middle forties at the end of the nineteenth century to over seventy today, the price increased also. The fact that the medicine and treatment that is needed can be ransomed when a person is ill has become the way of life. My sister and I were born at home, with the doctor traveling about ten miles to assist our mother. The cost was $20. This was in the late thirties, but just a few decades later my daughter was born in a hospital, and the fee was $100 for a general practitioner or $300 for the specialist plus $20 a day for the hospital. Fifty years later, this cost has risen to thousands, and you will not find a doctor to come to your house.

One of our local hospitals cost about $1,000 per day, and the other about $2,000. Both of these hospitals were non-profit institutions a few years ago, with one run by the county and the other a teaching hospital run by the state. Both are run by private corporations, and we see that nonhuman entity again. Within a hundred-mile radius, you can receive the best treatment for anything that may happen, including transplanting organs to replace those that have stopped working. What can be done is amazing. I have two cousins and a friend that are living with someone else's liver. What is the problem, then? The problem is that very few in our population can afford these treatments.

After I retired, I had to find a new physician and decided on an internist that worked for one of these new medical corporations. My first visit to get acquainted cost, $150 and there were no x-rays or tests done. My insurance paid nothing since it was an examination but did get a discount of about $60 for me. Of course if I had not had insurance, I would have had to pay the entire amount of $150. Again, the corporations are after the individual that has no weapons to fight back with other than to just not go to the doctor.

Another physician and I were discussing the cost of medicine, and he told me that if he could open a private practice and get paid $20 for each office call in cash, he could make more money than he does presently with a fee of over $100 per call. His cost of doing government and insurance company paper work plus the overhead caused by the necessity of facilities and equipment cost him the other $80.

A few years ago, a physician moved into the upstate New York area and set up a medical practice. He started charging about half of the fees charged by other physicians in the area. His admittance to the local hospital staff was blocked, and he could not treat patients there. This denial of privileges continued until his fees were the same as the rest of the local medical community. Apparently his abilities as a physician improved as he raised his fees. In many industries this is called price fixing, but not here. Offering to treat illnesses for less money made him an outcast in the medical community. Greed once more edged out the values of responsibility, honesty and compassion with the denial of a patient to choose his or her physician in the local hospital.

I have never thought that physicians should not be paid according to their skills and abilities, but the thought put forward that they should be paid for all of the experience they have is a misnomer. All of their experience was paid for, and many of their first patients did not receive the treatment of an experienced physician. The salaries of physicians are not the cause of the problems of rising medical costs in this country. In fact, the salaries of the physician's helpers, such as nurses and technicians, should be raised substantially. The increasing costs are associated with the old nonprofit institutions becoming for-profit. The hospital may not be for-profit, but the company brought in to run it is. Hospital administrators are making more than many of the physicians, and the profits for officers and stockholders has become more important than the practice of medicine. If you turn on your TV, you will find your local hospital and the pharmaceutical companies buying most of the advertising.

My local programming comes from Pittsburgh, and much of the local programming is paid for by the University of Pittsburgh Medical Center. Thousands of dollars are spent to advertise a hospital system and treatment centers. Where did the money come from to pay for this advertising? It came from yours and my insurance payments, Medicare payments and Medicaid payments.

I have wondered by how much room rates could be lowered if this advertising money was saved for the practice of medicine. I am not sure who the object of all of this advertising is for and why it is done. They have a captive audience, and to advertise for sick people to come to your hospital seems a trifle seedy to me. Perhaps Congress should make it a crime to use government program handouts to be used for frivolous uses such as advertising. The practice of medicine has lost its nobility and become like all other large corporations. "If you are sick and do not have any money or insurance, do not listen to our ads; they are not for you" is the message.

Another ad on TV every evening is for those motorized scooters and chairs. "Just call and tell us your problem, and we will try to extract the cost out of your federal government or insurance company." I am sure that there are people that need these for mobility, but why do I have to pay for them. These are not medical treatments, and their cost is greatly inflated to cover the cost of thousands of dollars in advertising. Again, why do we allow Medicare and insurance dollars intended for medical treatments to be used for advertising and private gain? This is one of the more blatant misuses of Medicare dollars I have seen since the most blatant misuses are hidden from view. Most of the rises in medical costs are for non-medical items and those associated with the delivery of items. "You will not have to go to the drug store for your supplies if you sign up for our services." Again Medicare pays for not only the supplies but also the delivery and the advertising involved.

The pharmaceutical companies have evolved from the snake oil sellers to some of the largest corporations in the world. The cost of drugs has risen much faster than the consumer price index, with many branded products having expected annual increases of ten to fifteen percent without any increase in cost. The branded companies price their new products according to their expected use to yield at lease one billion dollars in sales each year. The profit on most of these products is about eighty to ninety-five percent, with the payback for the research costs taking less than one year. We are told that about one third of the cost of branded products covers the cost of advertising, and here we go again with Medicaid and insurance dollars being used for advertising something that the patient cannot buy. "Tell your doctor that you want to try" whatever they are selling. You have noticed that branded pharma-ceuticals are paying for most of the television shows in the evening on two of the networks. You are paying for the cable to bring you the shows, and you are going to pay a premium for the drugs when you need them.

There is a controversy about going out of the country for your prescriptions because they are cheaper. One drug company threat-ened to stop deliveries to Canada to stop the flow of cheaper drugs to the USA if they fill prescriptions for non-Canadians. Why are they cheaper? The United States is about the only country that allows the free marketing of prescription pharmaceuticals in the world. If an American company sells drug products in England, the price is regulated to about half of that charged in the United States. The same is true for Germany, France and Canada along with many more. The pharmaceutical companies of the world come to the United States for their profits since they can charge anything they wish. A German company is free to charge what the market will bear here but is limited by price controls in Germany.

Since we have signed all of these so-called trade pacts that insist on freedom in the marketplace, it is unconscionable to allow foreign companies to charge Americans more for the same products that are under price controls in their home countries. Our health care system has not only become the golden goose for many in our own country but also has become a pot of gold for the foreign drug company. I wonder what would happen to the trade agreements if Congress passed a law limiting all drug pricing to that charged in a companies' home country.

I mention medicine in this book to put forth the fact that the noble practice of medicine that we believe every person should have access to has lost its nobility. The responsibility of the local hospital has been replaced by the need to make a profit, and the pilfering of the insurance and Medicare dollars intended to aid patients with the cost of medicine have shortchanged them. A lot of people and companies are getting rich off of the illnesses of the American citizen, and we seem helpless to do anything about it. The loss of values in the medical practice has reduced it from a profession to just another commodity that many cannot afford. What a shame that a society's responsibilities and honesty of purpose have been reduced to a television advertisement for more business.

Sports

The Greeks, then the Romans and now football, basketball, and so on. Sports invade our lives continuously from birth as the one entertainment that is available to all ages. From aerobics for mom to the Olympics, we participate in some sort of sports activity. Most of our sporting contests have become organized by community groups, schools, universities and for-profit groups and individuals. We grow up being taught that athletic contests are for participation and observation. Last evening I saw a TV spot on an elementary school in Chicago that used yoga to teach both exercise and meditation (yoga is a religious discipline and should not be allowed in a public high school). Trying to get the best of someone else or another team is taught as noble when performed in an arena for sport.

The gym in schools is the place most of us first learned how to participate in organized athletic contests. Those in the urban areas started organized sports outside the school with T-ball, football and basketball. A few years ago I had friends that hauled their ten-year-olds seventy or eighty miles away at 5 a.m. to play a hockey game. These children are being taught that winning is important and sportsmanship is expected. The athletic training is necessary for children to build strong bodies, and the sportsmanship builds character.

"What does this have to do with values?" you may ask. If you remember the hockey referee that was killed by an irate father in the Boston area a few years ago or the coach that was barred from coaching little league baseball, you should start to get the idea. Winning and beating someone for some has become the sport rather than the game, and when we start to teach our children that winning at any cost is the reason to play, we have breached a trust we have in the value system that is necessary for these children to become good citizens and leaders when they become adults. The good athlete plays, but the poor athlete sits on the bench and is taught that he or she is not equal to those that play all of the time. We were created equal, but not on the field of sports, and many times for young people this translates to other areas of their education and acceptance as an individual. The worship of the athlete has been started in the mind of the child and will follow them for the rest of their lives.

I just received the basketball schedule for my alma mater. The schedule is tough, but the most amazing part of the schedule was the cost of seeing a game. Three ticket prices that varied between league games and non-league games ranged from $18 to $65 per game and student tickets at $12 to $18 per game. The price list states further that better seats are available after an additional contribution to the athletic department. When I was a student, my tuition included tickets for football and basketball games, but now, after paying thousands in tuition, a student has to fork out the cost of two or three movie tickets to see their own team play. The games are no longer played for the student body but strictly for money. College sports have become pro sports, with the players being paid tuition and room and board. Imagine paying a teenager the same as you would a ranch hand and making millions from his or her efforts. It's a pretty good deal for colleges and universities, many of which are state institutions. The football team now represents the state, so there is no limit to the aid needed to beat the other state schools. Even with the states sponsoring their respective universities, the private institutions are keeping up with huge endowments and gifts. The athletic departments can raise money faster than any other department of the school. Our local university raised the salaries of the football coach and the basketball coach to more than triple the salaries of the people they replaced. While the president received a large raise this year, the professors and their assistants received a raise at about the cost of living index. Sports are much more important than academics, and keeping a coach is more important than keeping a top notch professor.

A few years ago I met a young professor of physics. He was taking flying lessons, and I was a flight instructor. We had many conversations about the university, and he told me that he would be here for three years. His last position was at MIT as he completed post doctoral work. He told me that his starting salary as a new professor was equal to what he would have received anywhere else but that in three years his salary here would be far below what he could command at other institutions. Three years later I met him as he was leaving town. I asked him where he was headed, and he said that he had been hired to join the physics department at Harvard. John said that he wanted to stay here but could not afford to live on what he was paid so had to move on. We had lost one of the best in his field, but we are not going to lose our football coach. Physics does not bring paying spectators so apparently is much less important than football. People will give money for the athletic department fundraising, but how many would give to increase the salary of a famous physics professor? Values! What is important in education to us? If we have children in the English or history departments, they become important, but to ask us to fund something other than the athletic department is just not in vogue.

The bowl games currently are being played, and millions of dollars are on the table for the teams playing. Our local team has left for its bowl, and many of my friends are getting ready to depart for the game. Most will travel by air, stay in a hotel for two or three nights and attend the game. They are spending thousands of dollars for these trips and write it off to entertainment. During the Christmas season, I wondered how many would support the needy and the hungry as well as they support the football team.

Professional sports have become a giant among the entertainment field, and the draw of the spectator has caused cities to spend millions for stadiums and arenas to reap some of the monetary rewards of the influx of fans. Pittsburgh had two referendums on the ballot for funding of a new football stadium and baseball stadium during the 1990s. Both were asking the taxpayers to help fund these projects, but both were voted down. The county went ahead and built them anyway with no regard to the wishes of the taxpayer. The lust of pro sports and their following became greater than the politicians' sworn duty to represent the people that voted them into office. I'm not sure that it was related, but this last year the state of Pennsylvania had to step in and help the city with their budget. It seems that the city had overspent and could not afford all that it was trying to do. Fiscal responsibility had also been cast aside. What is more amazing to me is that the same politicians are re-elected by the people that they ignored and put into debt. Values of responsibility and honesty and duty and respect disappeared when the thought of losing a sports team loomed.

The Pittsburgh professional hockey team has been left out

of the new arena syndrome but is insisting that either they get a new arena or they will leave. The same old blackmail is not working since there is no money left in the city's coffers. So the old sports nemesis is being sought to build the arena. That is gambling interests. Not so long ago, two professional football players were suspended for one year because they were betting on football games. Both were betting that their respective teams would win, so there was no way they would throw a game. The greatest hitter in baseball has been barred from the sport and denied a place in the baseball hall of fame. College presidents meet often to try to keep gambling out of their games and keep them above any suspicion of foul play. Now a sports team is asking to team up with a gambling operation to build them a new arena. By the way, they cannot fill the arena they are in now, but re-selling the box seats will bring a few more dollars. The idea of a sports team teaming up with a gambling concern is quite troubling to me, and I wonder what lesson our young hockey players will learn from this.

The cost of college and professional sports has risen constantly, with many professional players making millions of dollars a year with promises of more after retirement. To pay for this, ticket prices coupled with seat taxes have risen from a few hundred to many thousands of dollars. Television rights to broadcast games have continued to cost more with each new contract, with networks bidding against each other for those rights. The cost of television that used to be borne by advertising has become inadequate, and now part of that cost is being passed on to the cable or satellite subscriber. ESPN has raised its rates continually, and they have been passed on as increased cable rates, which for many people is just a tax for the rest of the channels they receive. Many do not watch or care for sporting contests but have to pay for them since ESPN is usually coupled with other channels that they do watch. To get them they have to pay for ESPN, which subsidizes the huge salaries given to the professional players and colleges. Most of the money for the arenas, stadiums and rinks used for sporting contests are being paid for by the tax payer without his consent. The Pittsburgh situation is a good example of this, and the taxes used to fund the two new stadiums could be used for many other needed projects. It is a fact in Pittsburgh that as the crime rate has risen, with drive-by shootings becoming daily occurrences, the police force has been reduced due to budgetary problems. Tax money for stadiums, but no tax money for police is the standard in many cities, as the thought of losing a team that fills restaurants and hotels on game day is more important than tranquility in the neighborhoods.

Sports and the lessons taught from participating in them have been and will always be an important part of our way of life. Promotion of sports for monetary gain has corrupted the very values taught by sports and turned them into vehicles for just another con game. Our taxes are misused, and the media has found ways to fund their enterprises by forcing many to buy and pay for entertainment items that they do not want. Monday Night Football just completed their last broadcast. Next year this thirty-six-year-old program will move to ESPN because ABC lost millions this year. Does this tell you anything about your cable or satellite rates next year? Somehow that huge amount of money lost this year will have to be made up. The cost of television viewing is going to increase once more to subsidize professional football. Values have been discarded for money, and greed wins once more.

Oil vs. Drugs

This past year we in the United States have seen drastic raises in the cost of energy in the form of petroleum and natural gas. The questions about this have been from greedy price gouging to the natural occurrence of free enterprise. I am not a lawyer nor have I ever studied the law and usually try to stay far away from this discipline, so the stories I am about to tell may not be legally correct. I will take that chance because if they are legally incorrect, they should be made correct.

We get our gasoline from a station that gets it from a distributor that gets it from a refinery that gets it from an oil well. There are thousands of oil wells around the world that supply this black substance that we have grown to rely on. These wells are located in South America, the North Sea, Alaska, the Gulf of Mexico, Texas, Oklahoma, the middle East and even in my state of West Virginia. These are a few places to find oil wells, and there are many more. The oil is purchased or produced by six or seven oil companies that serve the United States and is transported to their refineries. Out of the refineries we get the petroleum products for fuels, lubricants and chemicals. Many of the products that we use every day, such as the macadam that we drive on to the clothes that we wear, are made from these refined products. So from the thousands of wells to a few companies distributed to millions of consumers every day we can track the supply of oil. With all of this competition, how can the price of gasoline be raised twice in the same day at every pump in town when no gasoline was delivered that day to most of the stations?

The thousands of outlets for oil seem to put their product into a common pipeline, and one price is assigned without any competitive pressure on anyone. The oil business has become a monopoly in its distribution, and I thought there were laws against monopolies and price fixing. Apparently the laws that are on the books are either ignored or do not apply. You may have noticed that as companies get larger, they seem to avoid more and more regulation, which probably is directly related to their political giving. Thousands of oil wells and producers all charging the same price should tell us that something is wrong.

The hundreds of gas wells in my home state have not changed much except for new ones being drilled, but my natural gas costs have increased more than fifty percent in two years. Again, we are told that it is caused by shortages and free enterprise, but I have only one gas line into my house, and it is hooked to only one gas company. I do not have a choice from whom I purchase gas, and I am completely at the mercy of the gas company. My friends that own gas wells have not had any increase in their royalties as the prices have gone up, so apparently the money is going into someone's pocket.

Public utilities, and this should include many of the petroleum products, have become points of blackmail, and the American consumer has been the target. Giving up prescription drugs to heat your house should not have been necessary when the retirement you received a few years ago was adequate, but the utility companies and medical community have taken away your livelihood. We are told that there is no inflation, but I would welcome the person telling me this to pick up the tab for the increases in necessities that I am paying. How about home insurance that has raised three hundred percent, or natural gas that has raised fifty percent, or auto insurance that has raised twenty percent in the last three years? Somehow these items have not become part of the consumer's price index, and yet they rob many Americans of their chance of enjoying their retirement or sending their children to college. Greed with no controls and lack of respecting their customers has replaced the old fashioned customer service. The call to arms of many companies furnishing the necessities of life have been changed to, "Let's see how much we can get as soon as possible."

I want to tell you another story about a company raising its prices. Generic Pharmaceutical Company A received approval to ship Drug B to market. This company had proven that their copy of the branded drug was equivalent and had waited until the patent period had expired. The branded version sold for $1 per pill, and the new generic sold for seventy cents per pill. After some time, many other generic companies have received approval to make and ship the same Drug B. With the added competition, the price of the generic versions of Drug B had been eroded to six cents per pill. Because the generic companies started to lose money on this product, many stopped producing it. Company A found itself with one other generic company still making and shipping Drug B along with the branded version that still sold for $1 per pill. Company A's president told the sales staff to either raise the price for Drug B or stop selling it since it was losing money for the company. The sales department raised the price back to sixty cents per pill, or just below the price it had been introduced at. The consumer could buy Drug B from the branded company for $1 per pill or sixty cents per pill or from the other generic company at whatever they were charging.

There was an immediate outcry that Company A was price gouging, and the federal government brought charges against the company. Apparently Company A had also bought all of the raw material that one chemical company could produce so no one else could get any. There were many chemical companies that could produce this raw material but had ceased because they, too, were losing money and there was no market left. Following the government's law suit, twenty-six states sued under class action, and all of the sudden Company A was tied up in knots with law suits. Their attempts to do business were severely hampered by the legal problems, and after a year and a half they decided to settle for millions of dollars. I believe that if company A had been able to see the suits through the courts, they would have been vindicated, but the political and legal pressure was too much. Company A's only transgression was that they decided that since they had to answer to their stockholders, they needed to either make a profit on their products or stop making them. They were treated as a monopoly, but since there were two other outlets for Drug B, this was not true. It was true that many of the drug wholesalers and chains had not been passing the price erosion that had taken the price from seventy cents per pill down to six cents per pill on to the customer and were caught red handed with their respective hands in the till. These companies were not sued or prosecuted and had not broken any laws except the moral law of greed and deception.

Two events that caused anguish to many, but the larger oil companies were completely untouchable in their huge profit-taking scheme, and the generic drug company, in their attempt to keep a lower cost version on the market, was severely sanctioned. Guess who gives more money to politicians? Is this the answer? It is probably part of it, but also there is no commodity exchange for drugs, and there is for oil. One area in our capitalistic system is allowed to take the products of many and put them into one basket with one price. The difference between the original cost and the selling price becomes profit. This one stage in our economy acts as a monopoly but is not considered that way since it does not produce any products or services other than buy and sell futures on the products that we use or export. How thousands of oil producers can have their product gathered into one pipeline and hold the world hostage is beyond any form of monopoly that I know of. "Business as usual" is what we are told by our leaders, but try to tell that to Pharmaceutical Company A. A drug company that has excelled at keeping the price of medicine down to affordable prices is the one that is attacked because it is trying to make profit and stay in business while a few that produce nothing are controlling the price of oil and making huge profits at the expense of the American worker that cannot afford to drive to work anymore.

I think it is time for our Congress to reexamine what they believe monopolies are and what kind of laws are necessary to prevent one commodity from blackmailing us into poverty. In the case above the branded company was a foreign corporation. To sue one company for trying to sell its product at almost half of the brand company's price is an egregious act of differential control hysteria by our government and the politicians that run it. The complete lack of responsibility and honesty with the people that have elected these representatives is beyond any moral or ethical behavior and tells us that reelection and the campaign funds needed are much more important that any of our needs as citizens.

The capitalistic system works very well and has proven to be the best economic form of doing business, but with most freedoms comes responsibility. The business community has had regulations to force that responsibility upon it, and still parts of that community find ways to get around those regulations. If we go back to the discussion of corporations and the fact that a corporation cannot be sent to jail, we can understand why people running the giant companies are free to push the regulatory window. Lobbying and campaign funding has allowed this push to go unfettered until so many people are hurt that action has to be taken. Enron is an example of this, but just months before its bankruptcy, this company was the gleaming example of an American success story. There has been improvement in the sanctions of companies, with some of the most egregious acts bringing jail sentences to officers of those companies, but many are beyond the threat of sanctions by the control and power over us with their needed products, like oil.

Abortion

The defining subject in the selection of our judges and candidates for political office has been reduced to sexual freedom. Nothing about morals or ethical treatment or responsibility or honesty between parents and children is considered; only whether you are or are not for abortion. This subject has become more important to many than any other that should be considered in political races. The judge that is awaiting hearings in the Senate has one question to answer, and when he refuses, the same question will be asked in a thousand different ways. There will continue to be protestors carrying signs proclaiming that freedom for women means abortions on demand and also that abortion kills babies. Television and radio news and talk shows will discuss abortion over and over again, and we will hear both sides as hysterical rampages with no effort to put this candidate to the test of really understanding the Constitution of the United States of America. Unbiased law is no longer necessary, but being biased for or against abortion is necessary, which should be a disqualifier in itself.

What do you think about abortion? I have mulled this question over and over again in my mind and have yet come to a conclusion. There are some questions of values that are included in this discussion, and those are what I would like to talk about. My religion tells me that to abort a fetus is to kill a human being, and that is sinful, but is killing always wrong or sinful? I am still wondering about this but do know that there are moral and ethical laws that should govern any form of ending a human being's life.

In the early sixties I worked as a clinical chemist and medical technologist at an upstate New York hospital. One afternoon I had finished most of the day's testing when a stat request for a blood count, typing and cross match came into the laboratory. The order wanted two pints of blood as soon as possible, and we knew that someone's life was hanging on a thread. As I was not busy, I grabbed a collection tray and ran to the maternity ward to collect the blood samples necessary to complete the requested work. I was directed to put on a gown and scrub for three minutes so I could enter one of the delivery rooms to draw my sample. I entered the delivery room and started to put on the tourniquet when I saw for the first time the face of the patient. It was a teenaged woman whom I had known since she was a small child. She was trying to deliver a baby that had been fathered by her father and was having a difficult time in labor. I took my sample and ran to the lab to finish the requested testing and prepare the blood. The girl lived and went on to join the service and later marry. I saw her about ten years later, and she had grown into a beautiful woman with a handsome husband and was doing well. I thanked God for that, and yet today I still cannot get that moment when I recognized her out of my memory. If ever there was a need for an abortion I had seen it. Abortion was not legal at that time and was never considered, but that day I wished somehow that that beautiful young woman did not have to go through the trauma, pain and shame that had been forced upon her. For this reason and some of the other things I saw while working in the medical field, I have never been able to join my brothers and sisters in Christianity with the right to life movement, but I also will not join the opposite side, either. Both sides in this argument have left their values behind and think only about the power that they can yield with their zeal to further their position.

It is beyond my understanding that a young boy or girl are not allowed to carry an aspirin or Tylenol tablet to school with them but can meet in the locker room, conceive a baby and then go to an abortion clinic without notifying their parents. The people that are fighting for this are not from this planet, and I cannot start to understand the thought process that they use to formulate this kind of thinking. To strip parents of their parental rights and at the same time blame them for any transgressions perpetrated by their children is what you would expect from someone with a moron IQ. This is being fought for in the courts, and one case was before the Supreme Court on November, 2005. It was argued by Planned Parenthood of Northern New England against the Attorney General of New Hampshire. The decision was handed down on January 18, 2006 that reversed the District Court's permanent enjoinment of the statute which required parental notification before an abortion for minors and remanded any cases involving emergencies to a lower court. The women's rights movement, the ACLU and others believe that a child should have the right to get pregnant and abort the pregnancy at will without their parents having anything to say about it. What a way to teach our young responsibility, integrity, honesty, ethics and morality. All of these values are being thrown out of the window to perpetuate the idea of sexual freedom or using the act of procreation as entertainment and take no responsibility for your action. I call it the dog pack mentality, and the results are visible in our inner cities every day.

In the past few weeks a report on the number of abortions was made public, and the numbers are staggering, with the most occurring in New York. The number of abortions performed included many persons that received more than one abortion within the time period considered. Sex without responsibility is being pushed as a right by the agencies and groups that are Pro-Choice and against parental consent. Abortion rights activists claim it is also the responsibility of the taxpayer to cover the cost. I have almost come to tears thinking of the victims of this legislated crime that we have perpetuated on the very people that really need our help. I wonder if any of these young people will ever have a chance at a life that includes family and friends. Abortion on demand is treated as a right of every woman, and no one had ever trifle with this right, or you will be chastised by pickets and the secularists that have forced this horrible concept on us. The chance for the people that this practice is aimed at to ever learn a value system has been reduced to near zero, and yet we constantly are looking for ways to change the lives of the very people that we have deprived of this chance.

The people that are fighting to remove legal abortion have mostly been associated with the religious right and use Biblical text to back up their case. The fact that abortion is a medical procedure has not made it a medical decision but a political one. The doctor has been taken out of the equation and made an automaton that performs at the will of the patient. I have not been able to find a reason why any physician that has sworn to do nothing to harm life would perform abortions for birth control other than greed. To be trained as a physician and be able to heal the sick is one of the most noble professions, but then to turn your back on the training you received to become one whom ends life is beyond me.

The need to abort pregnancies has always been a tough decision for the doctor, and before the law allowed it, most were performed in secret. The fact that abortion is allowed today has removed this secrecy from the delivery room, but the number of medically needed abortions is very small next to the number performed to just make up for the mistake of unprotected sex. The right-to-life people have not considered the medical need for a procedure that may save the life of a mother. Allowing a pregnancy to continue after a rape or incestuous relationship should be a choice of the mother with the alternative of an abortion available.

The other side of the argument has been just as black and white in their case of abortion on demand without any parental notification. The women's groups try to further the idea that a woman is in control of her body and that no one other than her has the right to tell her how to handle her bodily functions. I suppose she can also cure her own diseases and fix any trauma she might receive. The mere fact that it takes two to tango should be applied here. A pregnancy just does not happen without a second person being close by, and parthenogenesis has not been reported lately. If a woman has control of her body, why, then, did she get pregnant in the first place? Apparently this idea of control is something that is used now and then and does not work during bad decision making. I do agree that a woman does have control over her body, but so does a man, and together they have the control that should prevent an unwanted pregnancy. Abortion on demand has made the male-female relationship just another flippant pleasure action with no thought of the relationship leading to the family situation to keep populating the world with responsible people. Responsibility, respect and learning how to start relationships in the future have been thrown aside to make the young girl free.

One of the things that we as a nation have been good at since the Second World War has been to keep our poor in their place, or maintain their poverty. We have taken the tack that to help the poor we have to provide them with what we deem they need. This has not included education, family values, respect, and doing what the mother robin does to her babies. We have not tried to teach the poor how to survive and compete for their fair share of the world's wealth and prosperity. As the mother robin kicks her progeny out of the nest to become a flying adult or just cat food, we have to teach, support and educate those whom are more unfortunate than we to fend for themselves. We have done the opposite, and abortion has furthered this notion that the poor are not capable to make the decisions of life. The idea of respecting one's body has been removed, and the need for responsibility in relationships has been overridden as unnecessary. Do not worry, because if you make a mistake, we will help with whatever you need. We have told the young person that they do not have to be responsible for their bodies and to just go out and have fun. When you get pregnant we will pay for an abortion, and you can start over again.

One of the most startling statistics to come out of the recent report on abortions was the number of procedures performed on the same teenager multiple times. How are we helping this young woman to become a self-sustaining citizen who can join those not suffering poverty? What do we or should we expect this young woman and her mate in the future to be as parents to the next generation? We have perpetuated the idea of poverty as incurable, and those suffering its effects are going to have to just get used to it. We will give you what we think you need, including abortions when you decide to use your bodies as pleasure machines without any responsibility for the outcome of your actions. We will continue to pay for all of what we deem necessary, and the vehicle you need to move out of your situation is your problem.

Stripping people of the values they need to start a healthy competition for their share of life is what we are doing, and the more we do it, the more we keep perpetuating their bane. I guess it is their right to stay poverty-stricken and allow us to keep on getting ours. Abortion has stripped away the values of respect for oneself and others. Control of one's body is worth the death of the next generation according to the pro-choice groups. I would say the need for abortion is caused by the fact that those that want it have lost control of their bodies and wish society to cure their ills. Many in our society have made the right to abortion a greater issue than any others to be considered by our politicians. Hunger, disease (except AIDS, which is another sexual freedom issue), jobs, the homeless, and access to medical care have taken a backseat to the argument for and against abortion. The dog pack sex mentality has become a way of life for many. It is sad that many dogs give us more respect than we give ourselves.

Race

How about race for a controversial subject? The subject that most of us will not or dare not discuss in public is the same subject that we all have very strong feelings about. This is what I think, but if I say anything about race, I will be politically incorrect. There will be an immediate response for or against my position, so keep quiet and get along. This permeates our society and has become another political football, with both parties saying that they are the party of diversity.

The racial problem in the United States can be broken into two areas, which are the matter of slavery and the idea that the color of one's skin places them in a higher or lower position in relation to their fellow humans. Slavery, which involves people of all races, has reduced peoples to a place just above animals for all of recorded history and continues today in various forms. How a person looks or appears to someone else has always instigated an immediate formation of opinion about the person, and we use ourselves to compare and contrast the differences. Are they fatter or skinnier than me, or are they prettier or more handsome than me, and on and on we go with our appraisal. The end result is usually wrong, and we find that out when we get to know them better.

Let us look at slavery and the effect on humans to understand a little of our history. Studies have been made and the history books written many times to answer some of the questions about the effects of slavery on a human being. Slavery in our country was unique. Most of the slavery in the world has come about through conquest by armed forces, with the people conquered being taken as slaves, whereas slavery in America was just kidnapping and enslavement. Most of recorded history tells us about the capture and enslavement of peoples, with the loss of their families, homes and value systems. Slaves have been used for everything from building the great pyramids to working in the houses of prostitution in our own day. Much of the Roman Empire was built by slaves. Cheap labor and entertainment created an environment that needed people that had no control of how they were to live and work. Today you can see the results of slavery when you travel to Egypt or to Rome. Some of the aqueducts built by the Romans are still in use, and the Roman iters, or roads are still indestructible today. Slavery built them all, and even with this legacy we still enslave people to do our hardest work.

The effort of people to escape their enslavement has caused some of the greatest moments in history, with the Bible telling us of the many battles fought to achieve this. The Hebrews' escape from Egypt is celebrated each year at Passover even though it happened thousands of years ago. Their escape from enslavement in Babylonia and subsequent capture by the Romans is a great part of the Biblical history presented to us as the foundations of a great religion. What is very interesting in the Bible is the fact that slavery is so prominent that we are told that, if we are slaves, we are to be good slaves, as though it is just an accepted way of life. Slavery did not end with the fall of the Roman Empire, and the spread of Christianity throughout the world has not stopped it. As they were driven from their land, the Jews were not all enslaved, but many became second class citizens in many countries as they tried to preserve their heritage and religion. As a people, the Jews have been chased, enslaved and killed for the last four thousand years, with suicide bombers still carrying out the continuation of this history. While we think slavery ended with the Civil War, we fail to open our eyes and realize that it has not ended. The Germans under Hitler enslaved millions to work in their war plants and then starved and killed all the Jews and others they considered religious zealots. It has been estimated that about one third of the Jewish population disappeared from the earth during the Second World War.

After this war and another freeing of an enslaved people, who would have ever thought that slavery was going to become another major item in the world? It was not until Solzhenitsyn wrote *The Gulag Archipelago* that we in the West started to understand that the USSR had enslaved its political prisoners and put them to work in labor camps under the cruelest conditions. Men and women were taken from their homes and families and transported to Siberia to work and spend twenty-year jail sentences in conditions that we would consider cruel for animals. Enslavement had again reared its evil head, and this time it was not any ethnic group or a different race but just the citizens of a country that had become so corrupt that preservation of the dictatorship was the only thing that mattered. As the world found out and started to raise objections, the brutality receded somewhat, but the lack of freedom to express oneself or to practice a religion was still denied. The enslavement was carried on until the breakup of the USSR many years later.

The one defining fact of slavery is that there is no escape. The Jews could not get away from the Egyptians, and the Russians could not escape to another country. Slavery robs people of many things, but most of all, it takes away the very things that we live for. Family, religion, education, and expression of thought are not needed by people that are treated as animals, and usually they are denied. Survival is the only reason to continue to live and strive for another day. When this treatment continues for generations, the education and values that are passed from parent to child are diminished as each generation passes until there is nothing left to pass on. When husbands and wives are torn apart or their children are taken from them, survival replaces the importance of family. Values that we take for granted have receded until they are no longer considered a part of living. Survival is the only thing left, and even that is left to the animal in us to make us breathe another breath. Hope is lost, and the idea of ever living any other way is not considered. The really sad part is that we are still allowing people to live in these conditions today and look the other way when it is before us.

You may disagree with me about the presence of this abomination being present today, but let us look at slavery in the terms of what it really is—the removal of freedom and the enforcement of the will of a stronger group on someone that is powerless to rebel. If you look at the enslavement of the African in the Americas and nearby islands, you will see a unique form of slavery in that the people enslaved were not conquered. Most of the Africans were kidnapped or turned over by rival tribes to Europeans that transported them to the New World to be sold. This practice of enslaving people was forced into the American economy, as it was still an English possession by the English and Dutch merchant marine. This slavery was different because the slaves had not been at war and had not been conquered by the people enslaving them. People that were from many different tribes and organized villages were ripped from anything they recognized and put aboard ships as cattle to be transported to a place they had never heard of. Many died during the trip, and the rest were treated worse than a farmer would treat his animals.

I have often wondered how the first African slaves learned to speak English as they were sold and put to work. It is beyond my imagination that any human being could treat another human being this way, but it still goes on as we try to raise ourselves above others. The fact that these people were black and looked different made it easier for their owners to forge a belief that they were less than humans. This was the way in which they were treated. The slave worked daily from dawn to dusk and in return received a place to sleep and some kind of food and clothing. He was not free to leave or to even voice his opinion in many cases. He received harsh punishment for the merest of offenses, many of which we would not consider as wrong.

Today we have people that are taking money from others that are desperate to leave their situation or country to get a chance in our country. They are transported across the border and dumped into a foreign land with no language skills or rights as a citizen. To find work, they have to accept the bottom wage, which is below the lawful minimum usually. After finding work, these people are forced to forge documents to get driver's licenses and other needed identification. Although this is voluntary by most of the illegal aliens and is not near the slavery we fought a war to rid ourselves of, it still comes near the indentured servitude that was present during the founding of our country. We have allowed a group of people to enter our country to work at the lowest wage to increase the profits of many, and it sounds pretty close to slavery to me.

The eastern part of the world is dealing in the trade of young women sold into slavery for the pleasure industry, but the most egregious situation is the fact that those that have escaped into freedom have not yet escaped the poverty they have been taught to live with. I'm not talking about the rest of the world but our own country. The poverty that people were put into one hundred and forty years ago as they expected freedom still exists today, and we as a society have worked very hard to prolong it.

When I first read a biography of Thomas Jefferson, I learned that he said the problem of slavery would have to be taken care of during the future generations. This admission told me that he knew that it was wrong, so why wait? Why would someone as brilliant and accomplished as him, along with John Adams whom also thought slavery was wrong, decide to wait another generation to do something about it? After reading a little farther and looking at the original first draft of the Declaration of Independence, I learned that Jefferson tried to do something about slavery when he wrote this famous document. He was ready to change the way this country treated all human beings. His declaration that all men were created equal was what he meant rather than that all white men were created equal. His attempts to further this idea met with stiff opposition from the Southern states since they were of the opinion that they could not survive without their slave labor. To keep the Union together, this half of the Declaration of Independence was omitted, and once again the slave issue was put off as he said for another generation.

Jefferson did free one of his slaves and had disastrous results when the young man could not make it alone. Freeing a slave could cost more than buying one, and the laws had been set up to make it almost impossible unless the owner was extremely wealthy. Slavery continued, and the African slave became worth three fifths of a white person when determining the number of representatives for each state to go to Congress. Can you imagine discussing what a human being was worth and coming up with a fraction for one race? The values that are supposed to be the glue of a society had left before our young nation was started.

The sixties brought about the change needed to allow this beautiful and talented people of color to once again try to establish themselves as citizens of a free country. The same freedoms that were guaranteed by the Constitution and Bill of Rights were within reach now, and it was time to fully become the equal of anyone and anybody.

Great social programs were instituted by the government to help this along, but if you look at these programs carefully, you will find they did just the opposite. Government housing was built as huge apartment buildings and welfare systems put in place to pay for food and clothing. Television sets became necessities, and travel by taxis was paid for when transportation was needed. These programs were put into place for the underprivileged in our society of which most were Americans of color that had been denied education, jobs and voting rights. Does this sound like anything that had happened before? How about no responsibility for food, clothing and shelter—just go to work? Instead of insisting on the responsibility of earning a living, the message was "stay in your new home and do not bother the rest of society." Stay in your little city within a city, and take what we give you, and do not cause us any more problems. Slavery had started all over again. Education was provided but at the lowest level because we have a habit of putting the best schools in the richest areas and the poorest schools in the poorest areas. Soon the values of responsibility, integrity, honesty and the work ethic that had built this country were diminished to the point that filling in time became the problem. Time was filled by forming street gangs and trashing schools along with disrespect for the rest of the world. The disrespect grew until killing each other became a way of life. Slavery had returned, and a people were suffering again.

I do not begin to think that I or many others that I know would have done a better job at assimilating the underprivileged and those born into poverty, which again includes people of all races and ethnicity. Surely someone should have stood up and said that there is no freedom and good life without responsibility, respect and courtesy to each other. The elected officials at the local, state and federal level seemed to be more interested in voter registration and party affiliation than insist on a good education and helping people to become self sustaining. The main attraction was the political power that was available to the party grabbing the most registrations. Today we see the results of our efforts, with many children raised by single mothers and grandparents, fathers more interested in their gangs and drug distribution than their responsibility for their offspring and young people that have been educated to believe that sex is for fun and pregnancy can be terminated at will. Responsibility for birth control, future pregnancies, some kind of family and earning a living have been replaced by liberal ideas that proscribe aid as removing the need for these values.

If all of the problems of poverty, segregation, racial prohibition and poll taxes were removed, maybe the color of one's skin or their ethnicity would mean less and allow all people to join in the American dream. This was the attempted result of the unrest and eventual legislation in the 1960s. Many doors were opened with the results of the demonstrations, riots and finally legal changes. But the American dream has still not happened for many, and as I have stated earlier that we seem to work very hard to maintain the status quo.

Former Mayor Berry of Washington, D.C., said that he was hurt because the hoodlums that robbed him at gunpoint did not recognize him as a friend. The former mayor thought that the robbers should identify with him as a friend and not rob him. December, 2005, Jessie Jackson led a memorial for an executed murderer that he thought should have been granted leniency. A few black leaders hold up as their heroes the very people that are robbing communities of their humanness, such as Tookie Williams at his execution on December 13, 2005, in California. Rappers, which are both black and white, are teaching our young people to hate policemen and misuse women.

The NAACP has politics and political power as its agenda, and if a black person is registered with the wrong party, they are not black anymore. Government thinks that the only answer is more aid or making college entrance easier. Jobs should be given to people because of need instead of qualifications. Everything that is needed to compete in society has been cheapened to the point that when something is difficult, such as admission to a professional school, it is immediately called racism. We have cheated people into thinking they have a right to anything they want because someone else has it rather than seeing that others have had to work for their share. As we have done in our education system, competing is not politically correct until it counts in the real world and we are not prepared. When we fail in our attempts at life, it is always someone else's fault.

Values, values and more values have been stripped and

replaced with gangs, drugs, promiscuity, and disrespect for one-self. The people and groups that want to erase racism and ethnic discrimination must first erase some of the problems causing it. My wife is of Italian descent. Her mother was from Italy and considered herself to be Italian. My wife considers herself to be Italian-American, and her son is just American. Why, then, are people descended from Africa more than two hundred years ago still calling themselves African American? Most of the Africans were brought to this country about the same time that my ancestors came. I never knew why my family moved out of Scotland until I saw the movie *Braveheart*. I figure that they lived in one of those mud huts and had their daughters ravaged by the Laird. Could be, but I have no knowledge of it. I am an American and cannot think of becoming a Scottish-American. I think it is time for people that have been in this country for over two hundred years of heritage to join us as Americans.

Injection of values into the poverty-stricken communities and looking up to those people that have become successful using a value system of respect and responsibility is closer to the solution needed. Hard work and education will not be replaced by government programs, and excuses of racial bias will not allow success. Those that make the excuses are maintaining the situation rather than helping it. The one thing that has amazed me is the fact that I have never heard of or read about others with dark complexions such as Indians, Pakistanis or North Africans complaining about racial bias preventing them from competing in our society. As a famous black actor told his interviewer, "If you do not see me as black, I will not see you as white." Simple and profound, but respect for each other as human beings may be the answer.

Press & Entertainment

We have discussed a couple of newspapers and their respective articles but have not really delved into the media as a whole. The values espoused by much of the media has contrasted rather than mirrored those of the American society. Our American society has become divided into groups that most think of as political groups but are really not about politics. The media, which includes the press and entertainment community, have taken a turn toward a form of secularism that cannot be defined by politics but rather by ethics and morality. Some politicians have joined with these entities because they represent a great deal of money and power. I have placed the press with the entertainment community because it is difficult to sometimes distinguish between the two. Much of the news we see is presented more as entertainment, and much of the entertainment is presented as political opinion.

The entertainment business has blossomed from the traveling minstrel and stage drama to everything from the balloon person for a child's birthday to a computerized movie. Television has put the entertainment industry into our homes and forced it to constantly find new ways to create revenue to fund it. The old stand-up comic and singer are no longer seen, but you can see autopsies being performed three days a week. The older family shows that were transferred from radio have been transformed into teenage dramas with lust, sex and bad language being used as the drawing point. News shows that are a hybrid of the press and entertainment industry have become nightly events with stories about crime, trials, and tribulations being screened as news. I used to think that these shows were factual and interesting until I saw one of the shows made. When the interviews and filming of the show was compared to that which was broadcast, it was a different show. The statements taped during the interviews had been edited and taken out of context, with the result being that of the network's expectations rather than the truth. The news show was just another entertainment presentation with a hidden agenda.

As we have progressed from the agrarian society of our fathers, we have found much more free time to fill with something other than work. Saturdays have become non-work days, and evenings have been opened to use for something other than work. Eight hour days and now even less have given us a lot of time to fill with entertainment and sports. Many of us have become accustomed to being entertained and find it hard to entertain ourselves, although that is the way that I grew up.

As a young man, it was up to me and my friends to entertain ourselves when time permitted. There were always the assigned chores and errands. But after those were finished, we filled time with homemade games of cops and robbers, cowboys and Indians, baseball on the town common and camping in the woods. Many a time we made bows and arrows out of willow branches and cattails to hunt for rabbits. We never hit anything, but at the time we were great hunters. As time went on, the idea of children having to create their own playthings was replaced by television and Toys R Us. We became a generation of fun and games without having to do very much. Everything was done for us, and the easy life had started for many. From Howdy Doodie to Mister

Rogers, we were entertained and later educated by the television. The so-called adult shows progressed from *Arthur Godfrey* to *Sex and the City,* and away we went into the sunset with any form of ethics left behind. If it feels good, it must be good, and this has started to rule the entertainment business.

The use of offensive words has progressed from "egad" to anything and everything including vulgarity. Swearing and the use of descriptions of anatomical functions that are not the ones in the text books have become commonplace, with good English replaced with slang and colloquialisms. The amount of skin shown has increased until all but five square inches can be seen on a woman's anatomy. Each new movie has to contain at least one sex act, and the story line is often left while the sex is portrayed. I am in the process of submitting a novel to a publisher and have been told the agent will not use some publishers because there is no sex in the novel. The incorporation of sex in a drama that is not about human relationships is a common occurrence, and many times one might wonder what happened to the story. Entertainment tries to sell the idea that it is mimicking society, but our society would crumble if it acted as it is represented. The dog pack sexual mentality is forced upon us constantly, with a horrible educational effect on youngsters. Picking up a gun and using it to settle an argument has been transposed to children and gangs as the method of choice. Proving manhood or womanhood with chest pounding and sexual conquests is the way to go according to the evening sitcoms and movies. The superman ideology of muscle and weapons is taught as the ultimate goal for all young men to reach for. Sexual conquests and winning the local tough guy contests to make us successful as humans are demonstrated in much of the entertainment available, with morals and ethics forgotten. The thought of injecting religion into a drama with a positive spin is now unheard of, and when a religious movie depicting the killing of Jesus was made, the entire Hollywood community turned its back and rejected the project. Its distribution was rejected, and many of the television presses made light of the religious history being portrayed. If a clergyman of the Christian or Hebrew faith is included in a drama, it is usually in a negative role.

With the anti-religious action the secular community, which is comprised mostly of the press and entertainment establishments, is the rejection of the Constitutional guarantee of religious freedom. It is politically incorrect to talk about one's religion in public discourse, and surely being on the side of good in good versus evil is just not in vogue. The accused is the one being harassed by the police and criminal justice system, and the victim is without sympathy. Movies and television shows constantly depict criminals as heroes and the rule of law as unjust and biased. There have been many dramas of late that depict the religious right of Nazis and racists, with the Gospels of the Bible used to back their claims. One movie for television had a Catholic Priest as the murderer and the alter boy as the victim. Pushing an agenda of freedom to do anything that feels good is not to be tested by the ethics and morality taught in a church.

Some have called this an attack on Christianity, and a book was published about the secular anti-Christmas movement. Stores and merchants were removing any reference to Christmas and replacing it with the word "holiday." Selling Christmas gifts for profit was good, but calling it Christmas shopping was politically incorrect. I disagree with the attacks on Christianity being the agenda, but rather, the attack is on the very ethics and morals that should prevent each of us from misusing others. The respect of one's body or the body of another or marriage between a man and a woman with vows that really mean something go against the values being sold by Hollywood. Family values that require parents to take care of their children and accept the responsibility of bringing them into the world are required only if living in a middle class area. The poor are being ill-treated if it is expected that they act in a responsible way, and the rich turn their parental duties over to the nanny.

The attack on religion is partially true because of it being the last place to find an attempt to teach morals and ethics, but disturbing the "feel-good attitude" is the most egregious act against the entertainment industry. The idea of marriage lasting a lifetime, sex being thought of as a method of procreation or education incorporating ideas other than liberalism that stand up to the ideals of the major religions of the world are to be dismissed from society. The new sin of Hollywood is to believe in and support a religion with values that go against the fun and games of a spoiled and uneducated society that exists in a world of make-believe.

One of the most interesting ideas put forth by the entertainment industry is their interest in politics and the liberal ideas they sponsor. Gun control is usually at the top of their list, and I laugh at every mention of this as it is promoted. For Hollywood to want guns controlled and removed from society at the same time they are training our young how to obtain and use them is quite hysterical. The Saturday morning cartoons kill more people per minute than any war has, and each evening we see shooting and knifing and strangling constantly. You cannot find very much in the way of entertainment without sex or crime involved, yet we should remove guns from society. There are a few dramas that try to show the sin of owning or selling a firearm, and usually the good guys are the bad ones in this type of presentation. We see the gang members being heroes and the bank robber justified by the way society has treated him and good and bad being switched for the sake of a political message or a challenge of authority. The rule of law is very seldom the rule of a moral people but of tyrants.

After working and going to school for many years to educate myself about the world and its wonders, it is really amazing that a good looking body or a lilting singing voice can all of the sudden propel a person to the specialist category in politics, religion and world affairs. People that have made a lot of money with their talent or body seem to think that they have become educated because of their riches. Some have taken the time to educate themselves in colleges and universities, but these are not the people that we hear ranting and raving about being politically right. The entertainment community lives in a society of make-believe where lying with a straight face is worth millions. This place in which dreams become realities and good can be portrayed as evil becomes the way of life for many. Over the rainbow is reality, and the real problems facing our society are beyond comprehension; but the lessons of this make-believe world is the basis of the entertainer's politics and religion. Their power is derived from the fame of their craft and is transposed as intelligence as it is forced into our homes every day as various agendas are pushed. Religion gets in their way, so it is pushed aside as politically incorrect. It is replaced with same-sex marriage and union, living together without marriage, making out criminals as tortured persons, asking judges to legislate that which the majority of citizens will not and using name-calling to replace intelligent discussion and argument. The absence of education and intelligent discussion is replaced with charisma, nice faces, well-built bodies and television presentation with backup supporters. The agenda is usually against someone rather than for an ideal or positive action. The only thing that I find more depressing than an actor or singer trying to be political is a college professor that does not know what narrow-mindedness is.

The press is in the same pickle as the entertainment industry because they use the same tactics to get our attention. The problem is that our country needs a strong honest press corps to balance the political power of those in government. The Constitution gives the press a freedom that is denied in any other country. The freedom granted to the press is one of the most important parts of the Constitution, and with it comes great responsibility.

Two years ago I was in St. Andrews, Scotland, to play golf on those old and famous courses. One day our group traveled out of town and played one of the newer courses. My caddie was a young man that attended the same university that English royalty was attending, and as we talked, he told me that he did not know the prince but that if he did it would be expulsion for him if he discussed anything about him. He also said that by law there was nothing printed about the royal family without permission in the United Kingdom. The press in England is not free. Our free press is taken for granted without realizing that it is a precious gift given to us by our founders. The misuse of the press to forward agendas or favor one political party is an egregious act of irresponsibility and starts to crumble the very basis of the need for a free press.

Yesterday the news put forth included the National Organization of Women's call for the termination of Joe Paterno as head football coach at Penn State because his comments about a young football player's suspension for sexual assault were not as they wished. Joe had talked from the player's point of view, and the NOW wanted the victim's point of view. There had been no arrest, and the rest of the story was omitted. At the same time a judge in Vermont had sentenced a man to sixty days in jail for raping a little girl from the time she was seven years old and for the next four years. I heard about this on only one news channel, and there was no attempt by the media to report or question the treatment of this victim. Apparently the judge was a liberal, and that made it all right, but Joe's action was against a liberal, so it was wrong. The press had a chance to bring a tragedy to light, but they preferred to advance the agenda of a group that has forgotten women and taken up politics instead. A non-arrest was worse than the rape of a child, and the hypocrisy of the press was in full view once more.

A mine explosion in West Virginia caused the deaths of twelve miners, and the news coverage was intense. All of the major networks were at the site and reporting around the clock as we waited to see if the trapped miners could be rescued. There were constant interviews of relatives, employees and company people to keep us abreast of the situation. One evening it was reported that the rescue crew would reach those trapped later in the evening, and I went to bed believing that by morning we would know the outcome. The next morning I retrieved the newspaper from my front porch and saw the headline reporting all twelve alive. I said, "Thank you, God" and proceeded to leave for my morning coffee shop. The thing I noticed about the headline was that it had been written, as Mr. Nichols had taught me in journalism class, with the most important thing first, then the next most important thing. When I got to the shop, my friends asked what I thought about the miners being found dead with one only one alive. I lost my breath as I tried to put what I had read with what I was being told. The newspaper had got it wrong, and so did the *USA Today* and many others. The news had become a necessity to get a scoop rather than the truth. No one at the site had bothered to ask the company to confirm or deny the rumor that the miners had been found alive. The rumor was printed to be first.

That morning I saw the morning shows on television as I did my exercise on a treadmill at a local gym, and the NBC show had Matt Lauer on from West Virginia. He was unshaven and reported that he had left New York at three in the morning to get to the site. I could not believe what I was hearing. All of the miners but one were dead, so what was there to report on and why travel after the drama was over? Apparently there was advertising to sell and money to be made on the misery of the miner's relatives through interviews of the families and friends.

It became clear that the news media was about to place the blame of the tragedy on the company and single out the person most responsible. The next day Brian Ross from ABC interviewed the CEO of the mining company and proceeded to ask him questions about the compensation for the families. As the man started to answer, Brian cut him short and answered for him, then asked how much of his own money was offered. He was portrayed as this very wealthy person that was making his fortune on the backs of the poor miners and then not caring about their families after the accident. He said over and over again that the owner was a billionaire. Rather than trying to interview a grieving person and find out pertinent information about the future of the mine and its employees, Mr. Ross had already indicted and convicted the owner. Mr. Ross was a disgrace to the profession to which he belongs, and the freedom granted to the press was misused once more.

Somehow a degree in journalism or English is transposed to doctor, lawyer, politician, governor and president. Science becomes a specialty, and convicting or freeing a felon before the jury hears the case is just another of the benefits of journalism school. Just as the actors and singers become experts, reporters have assumed the same power as they become more popular and command more money. Millions of dollars in salary for someone to read the news each evening is insane, and when you receive this kind of compensation, I guess it is easy to assume that you are pretty smart about all things. The sad reality was that the reporter telling us about the miner being transported to Pittsburgh for treatment in a hyperbolic chamber got his chambers messed up. It was a hyperbaric chamber, and efforts to explain its use were horrible. The morning show on Fox reported that the living miner had carbon monoxide in his blood when tested but that they could not tell how much had been present before his rescue since he had been receiving oxygen. After this report, Steve Doocy reported that there was no carbon monoxide present in the miner's blood. Apparently he does not listen to his own news casts. Show time is more important than truth. Mixing entertainment and news coverage dilutes both to just plain gibberish.

Most of the day's news can be read or told in a few minutes, but the telecast is longer than that. The news channel is reporting news twenty-four hours a day. It does not take long for these broadcasts to run out of news, or at least the news that fits their agendas. The liberal bias is very prevalent in most news media, and favoring the Democratic Party is close to campaigning. Some networks should be offering equal time to the opposing party or listing part of their broadcasts as campaign contributions. After the real news is read, something else is needed to fill the time slots to continue to sell advertising.

During the Viet Nam War, CBS was found to stage mock battles to enhance their evening news. They were trying to illustrate what the war was about. Some of the other news outlets are still creating stories. Most are not as much false but non-stories that have some form of sensationalism added to them. A writer for the New York Times confessed to making up stories to enhance his career, and it would be interesting how many others are enhancing their stories for the same reason.

The news channels have morning shows that mix news and social items with entertainment and reviews of books and sports events. These shows used to be carried with one or two people, with the sports person or news person coming in to report in their area. The anchors sat at a desk or table and basically entertained us as we heard the news, scores and weather. Now there are usually three anchors, of which at least one is female with a short skirt and no desks or tables. I finally started to believe that these networks think that men will watch, waiting for the Sharon Stone moment as she portrayed it in *Basic Instinct*. Sex sells, and why not use it on the morning news show? Watching a good looking woman tugging at her skirt and trying to be somewhat sophisticated at the same time is pretty funny, but why put her in that position in the first place? Of course you cannot find any people on these shows that are not good looking, and the plain Janes should not apply. The news has become entertainment, and the mix has led us to be very wary of the truth of that which is broadcasted. Ratings and agendas are the important items, with what is happening in the world taking second place. The news of the Iraq war always starts with the number killed and many times stops before anything positive can be iterated. It would be great if we could see what our troops are doing in Iraq besides being killed and why they come home to proclaim that they made a difference and are ready to go back.

The New York Times reported that the president has authorized the NSA to listen to telephone conversations between known terrorists abroad and citizens in the United States. This was called a horrible misuse of executive power, and Bush was out of line once more or something like this. Again, there were many areas to examine here, with the first being who leaked the story to the paper, and second, why did the paper wait for one year to publish the story, and did the president really misuse his powers? Rather than try to examine these questions again, I would like to compare the actions of the president to the press as they pursue a story.

Invasion of privacy is abusive behavior any time, but what is privacy and what is public? The press has decided that any time they can stick a microphone into one's face, the moment is public. Many times we see reporters knocking on the doors of people's houses to ask questions or parking television trucks on the street in front of someone's home to get a story.

This last year there were two trials, one of which was for murder and the other sexual abuse. The television and print media were camped at both sites for that up-to-the-minute report. The defendants were tried each evening on the news, and both were convicted before the jury had been introduced. When Michael Jackson was acquitted, it did not fit with the media's expectations, and this was made known. Why the news cannot be limited to the fact that there is a trial and then the final outcome is beyond me. The press is willing to turn someone's agony into a soap opera for a story they believe will attract readers, listeners and viewers. The show must go on and on and on with no regard to the psychological effect on the defendants or victims. The young lady that accused the basketball player of rape was raped again by the press and then again by the criminal justice system. Our right to know is being pushed a little further than necessary, but let the victims of this overexposure fall as the press keeps its ratings and advertisers. I would rather the president listen in when a terrorist calls me than have a reporter stick a camera in my face when I am facing a heart-wrenching situation. Showing a grieving mother or wife or child is not what I call good journalism.

The freedom guaranteed to the press by the Constitution is one of the most amazing freedoms ever given by a government to police those running the same government. The responsibility that goes along with this freedom is tremendous and should always be taken as duty to country. The protection of sources and reporting crimes against the state are a part of this freedom and responsibility. I am not sure where that reporting responsibility and the responsibility of citizenship are separated. We have seen the press in this country take sides against us and support foreign ideals to prove that they are objective and refuse to stand up as citizens when their knowledge could solve crime. The freedom to protect sources as a lawyer protects his client with privileged communication or the secrecy of the Catholic confessional has many times allowed treason to go unpunished and terrible crimes to not be solved. This area of law is not something that I feel qualified to make decisions about, but I do wonder why we as a nation do not define the limits better.

The press has a huge job to do and must return to accurate reporting with the political and religious bias left at home. When important news is slanted to favor a special interest, the news becomes false and has no value, as the reporter becomes just another writer of novels. Many in this country have become very suspicious of the information given as news, and as newspapers and network television continue to put out their biases, they also continue to lose subscribers and listeners. The press should be holding all political parties and all politicians up to scrutiny and refuse to be bought and paid for by any special interest group. The press corps needs to return to the values of integrity and honesty and respect their readers and viewers as people who are as educated as they are. The idea that the people in the entertainment and press industry are somehow superior in knowledge is going to be a problem until they have a chance to live and work with the people they expect to pay their way. They instead place themselves above others in their own minds.

Let's get with it, because we need you badly.

Politics

What a word this is! The sound of it evokes emotions, and usually they are suspicious and wary. We associate politics with running for a governmental office at the local, state or federal level.

As a young man, I joined the Young Republicans and worked for the election of Barry Goldwater for president. Our man lost, but I received an education that is still with me. Meeting the leaders of the local party and working with them soon had me realizing that political power starts at the lowest level. The area was central New York, which is very Republican but quite liberal, and because of this, the leaders of the Republican Party were very powerful, as they selected the people running for all of the local offices. The national political arena was important to me, but to affect anything beyond the local level, you had to advance in the leadership levels at home. We lost the national election by a landslide and won all of the local seats, and my idealism was corroded by the lust for the power of running a county. Since that time, I have not participated as a member of any political party in a working sense. As I look back on that experience, it is easy to figure out why many good and qualified people do not run for office. The maneuvering through the political machines is next to impossible unless you are willing to compromise your ideals. Power is held by many and at various levels, with each wanting something in return for their support. "You pat my back, and I will pat yours" is the way through the maelstrom of the political swamp that each candidate has to swim through. I had had enough just looking at it without jumping into the mud and trying to swim.

If we look at the history of our country, we will see politics starting as soon as the first Continental Congress met. Of course there were political battles for seats in each colonies' governments, but these were subjected to the oversight of the English. We have already mentioned the battle over who was free and equal under the law, and the next big battle came during the forming of the Constitution. Ben Franklin supposedly held up progress on the Constitution over the matter of compensation of those holding seats in the Congress. Ben wanted no pay or to have these members serve at will, as he said paying them will cause corruption. Of course he lost this battle, but his words still haunt me and many others when we see our representatives and senators raising their pay and granting themselves a retirement plan second to none. The thought of money becoming a factor of how well the future Congresses would perform should not have been that hard to imagine, but Franklin was overruled.

The first large battle over the philosophies that differentiate our main political parties started as the Constitution was being written. The role of government and how it governed was in dispute, with one side believing that the common man was not capable of participating and taking part in the government's actions, while the other side was wary of government and thought it should do no more than was necessary and include all citizens. The great battle was between Adams and Jefferson and then Burr and Hamilton joined in with Madison and others following. The first fight was about the roll of the president, with Adams wanting this role to be much like the King's role in England; but Jefferson protested that the president should not be in an office held for life or handed down to family. We see the philosophy of small government against big government as the basis for the Republican and Democratic parties today, but most of us do not see it in their actions. A couple of weeks ago, I heard a television talk show host who portrayed himself as a liberal say that government was too big and should be made smaller. His statement came out of the campaign that I worked on for Barry Goldwater, who was an avowed conservative. While this host calls himself a liberal, I do not believe that he knows what a liberal or conservative is.

The philosophy of the candidate usually lasts until election, but then it is off and running to get re-elected, and philosophies are out the window. Politicians have made the election process full time with very little time left to do the jobs they were elected to do. Campaigns have become full time money raising events, and the people that actually vote for a candidate are important at election time only.

This past election for president found my state of West Virginia favoring Bush over Kerry with a majority of popular votes. The electoral votes of my state were cast for Bush. Our two senators are Democrats and have been elected many times by the same people that voted for Bush. One would think that if the people voted for you and had also voted for a particular person for president, the message should be that the people you represent wish to go toward the President's vision. Is that confusing? If I vote for Senator Byrd and President Bush, am I not telling both of them to get along and represent me in the way they have campaigned? Of course you know the answer is that Byrd and Rockefeller have not received the message and have taken the tract to oppose the president on each matter before him. These senators have performed in a manner opposite from that which the majority of voters in my state requested, and I feel that they have thumbed their noses at us with no shame. Their goal became the election of a Democrat to the presidency and had decided to start immediately instead of carrying out the work needed to win a war or aid the economy or even to raise the state of West Virginia above the forth-eighth place out of fifty in most categories. The campaign has started, and anything that we had supported the president for has become a negative action for these two senators. Politics is alive and well.

West Virginia is my adopted state, and I have grown to love it and the people in it. But! We are last in many categories of economy, taxation methods, jobs, average income, education, health care and for a while had the distinction of being the fattest.

After moving from New York, where manufacturing and service companies were being driven away by excessive taxes and regulation, I found that an outdated tax system and the lack of regulation was preventing those jobs leaving New York from moving in with me. Instead they were going farther south to North and South Carolina, where changes had been made to the corporate environment. My home was in a city that was also home to West Virginia University and not a good example of the rest of the state. Most jobs in my city were and still are government jobs with the state run university, NIOSH, Department of Energy and the Medical school associated hospital. Senator Byrd is spoken of with reverence because of the gifts of federal money, and many of the institutions and buildings are named after him. He has been buying votes for a long time and seems to be paid up for the next election. Most of the projects he has helped to fund are good and needed but are not job creators for the private sector. With all of the federal dollars that have been spent on our state, we are still near the bottom of the wage scale and have many residents existing at or below the poverty level.

The dollars that most states receive as pork are in the same category as our gifts from Byrd in that they buy votes but do not further the education systems or economies of those states; rather, they are like Medicare and student loans. These gifts become relied upon, and soon we are not trying to help ourselves but looking at our politicians to pay our way. Many of the dollars from Senator Byrd have been noble gestures, such as the new Cancer Center and an Alzheimer research center, but very few have helped the state with the infrastructure that we are missing.

There is a small city south of Morgantown called Fairmont, which is located on interstate 79. When the interstate was built, there were three exits to access this city, which is the home to Fairmont State University. A few years ago, another exit was built, but I have yet to find anyone that can tell me why. The fifth exit to this city is under construction now and should be finished this summer. Why is this important? It is pork. The Congressman from our area has decided that he needs to keep pouring money into the Fairmont area and apparently buy votes for the next election. I say this because just north of Morgantown there is a road project that has been in progress for ten years that will connect our area to Pittsburgh with four lanes. At present, a small country road is the major route from much of the Pittsburgh area to West Virginia and is full of tractor-trailers daily. Money for this road has been unavailable at the state or local level, and the need for federal dollars is quite apparent. Rather than increase the commerce between a large city and West Virginia that would open markets for our services and goods, this Congressman is buying votes by adding a fifth exit from an interstate to a small city with no benefit other than the construction jobs it has offered. The unions will endorse him once again.

When the two-party system is working, both parties have to perform to stay in power. When an area, such as central New York State that is predominately Republican or West Virginia that is predominately Democrat, power is easily maintained for the party in power. This is West Virginia with a predominance of registered Democrats. Although the state is conservative in many areas, the party machine is so powerful that competition happens only at the primary level of voting. The result of this dominance is the lack of performance of our legislators in building the infrastructure and tax systems that will attract new business.

I mention the tax system because when I first moved here and bought a house, I found out within the year that the tax system was more like that in Sherwood Forest during Robin Hood's day. The sheriff collects the taxes, and when you buy a piece of property, the name of the owner is not updated with the tax notices still going to the former owner. This happened to me, and the former owner happened to move to Florida. He did not forward the notice to me and I found out about the tax bill a week before my house was to be auctioned on the court house square. Other taxes are what I would call business preventers, as they tax the losses as well as the profits. The predominance of one party has allowed this to continue because it is just easier to get reelected if there is no pain such as that when a change in the tax system is started. Many West Virginians have been conditioned to expect their elected officials to take care of them just as the inner city poor expect government to pay their living expenses. Bringing in federal dollars is more important than changing the tax laws and tort system to allow growth through private enterprise.

We see the problems of my state happening at every level of government as politicians get elected and start working for reelection immediately instead of tackling the difficult problems that could solve problems for future generations. Social Security is one of the problems that needs to be fixed, but to do so will cost some politicians their seats. And solving problems has become the farthest from the job of the elected official. Increasing power and pay for themselves is more important than helping their constituents to do the same. Much of the behind-the-scene schemes of amendments and earmarks that are used by Congress to reward special interests would be considered criminal if the same were done in the private sector. Lobbying and special interests are the huge pot of gold that each politician looks to for help at election time.

We have a tax in West Virginia called the B&O tax, or Business & Occupation Tax. It is levied on businesses and is paid on the gross receipts. Years ago I bought an airplane, and to aid in paying for the maintenance and storage, I leased it to the local flying business for which I worked. Because I had a lease agreement (it was oral), I had to get a business license, file state sales tax reports and pay the B&O tax on my receipts. I never came close to making a profit, but the tax was due quarterly and had to be paid. I mention this tax because it is regressive to business, especially new businesses that have to pay it on gross receipts before they have started to be profitable. Another example of this tax was when I built a new home within the city. The general contractor had to pay the B&O tax, as did his subcontractors, which amounted to double taxation on my new home. The city and county live off of this tax and refrain to use zoning or building codes to control construction and development that would slow the flow of B&O taxes. Raising other taxes to replace this tax would possibly cause some of them to lose their seats on the city council or the county commission.

Every day politics and the causes and effects of political actions are thrust into our lives, the latest being the actions of the Senate and a bill passed in Maryland and promoted in West Virginia regarding Wal-Mart. The United States Senate is the most powerful and prestigious governmental body in the world but has shown itself to be lacking in the values we think of as the glue of civility. Their actions as they questioned Mr. Alito about his qualifications for the Supreme Court were an absolute embarrassment that was available for the rest of the world to see. Attacking a good and decent citizen with his family present in front of the world for political gain was outrageous and showed everyone that we are capable of electing very unprincipled people to the highest offices in the land. One senator read from a prepared note that he could not support the nominee and gave the narrowest of reasons why. The impropriety of writing a smearing dismissal of Mr. Alito before he had finished his questions tells us all that whatever was said, his vote had been bought before the committee's action began. What a shame that the world had to see this. It is no wonder that the rest of the world does not respect us as we wish. The misuse of a human being in the United States Senate for all to see is an ugly part of our political system.

The reason for the negativity of some senators toward this candidate was his expected views on abortion. Sexual freedom, or the right to sex without responsibility, was the main reason to not support Mr. Alito. It was as if the candidate that was supposed to demonstrate his absence of bias could not be confirmed unless he possessed the right kind of bias. To be accepted, he would have had to demonstrate a reason to be rejected. One small subject that should not be in the hands of the courts or the legislature but in the hands of the medical profession was the only matter considered. The narrow-mindedness of these interrogators and their lack of responsibility, respect and honesty is a travesty, and why and how people such as this keep getting elected demonstrates how apathetic and unthinking we as the voting public are. To place blame without including our responsibility as voters is in itself irresponsible.

The other effect mentioned is the state of Maryland passing legislation to force Wal-Mart to provide a minimum amount of health insurance for their employees. The West Virginia legislature has been contemplating the same action. Can you believe that a law was passed that virtually tells Wal-Mart how they have to handle their employee benefit plan? I certainly do not believe that it is Constitutional to tell a private company how to run its benefit and compensation plans other than to insure adherence to minimum wage guidelines. The legislation was pushed by the labor unions because of their inability to organize Wal-Mart. Apparently the employees of Wal-Mart are happy as non-union members, and the unions see a huge pot of gold in the expected dues from a unionized Wal-Mart. Attacking a company that has provided thousands of jobs and low cost goods because unions wish to increase their dues take is not about helping the worker but about power and wealth. This power and wealth is then translated to political power since the dues collected from any organization of Wal-Mart would in part be given to the Democratic Party to elect their candidates. Indirectly, the Maryland legislature has passed a law to increase their chances of receiving more campaign funds from the labor unions for the Democrat Party members. Special interests are more important than the thousands of workers at Wal-Mart, and those workers are being harassed by the very government they elected to protect them.

People running for election to an office go to the voting public and ask for support in return for the kind of representation offered. This has become a very costly business, and raising the funds to campaign has become a year-long endeavor. Most of the funds come from businesses and special interest groups and not the supporting voters. As soon as the person has been sworn in, his or her allegiance changes from the voter to the very special interests that he needs for the next election.

A few years ago, as the GATT treaty had been ratified by the United States Senate, it was found that one provision extended the patent life of some products up to two years beyond that intended or legally given. The Senate was going to fix this provision and return the patent lives to that which had been proscribed by law before the treaty. Some of the products affected were pharmaceuticals, and one of the drugs was grossing over two billion dollars a year in the United States for the company holding the patent. When the fix was enacted, this company was going to lose two years of patent life, at which time a cheaper generic version would be available. After this company spent millions of dollars on lobbyists and reelection campaigns, the Senate held up its vote long enough to find enough votes to keep the provision as it was. The company went on to sell their drug product in the United States for two more years for more than four billion dollars. The consumers of this drug (a group of which I was a part) had to pay more than double for it because the United States Senate had been bought by a pharmaceutical company. Are you ready for this? The pharmaceutical company was a foreign company that happened to have a manufacturing plant in one senator's district. For the love of money and bowing to special interests, the senators that we elected turned their collective backs on the American public to aid a foreign company because it would help each senator with a branded pharmaceutical company in their state.

Every year someone or some group tries to change the way we elect our government officials with all sorts of campaign reform. The last attempt made the special interest group more powerful instead of preventing it. The last presidential campaign was bombarded by advertisements supporting one person or another, and while they spent millions of dollars, none of these groups could vote. The only way to bring our representatives back to the job for which they have been sent to do is to restrict campaign contributions to be given by those that are registered to vote and no other group or corporation. The attacks on Wal-Mart by a government for the special interest of organized labor would cease and real, legislation addressing the problem causing the high cost and unavailability of medical care could be considered instead.

Would it not be wonderful to think that your elected representative would welcome you into his or her office as quickly as the lobbyist or corporate executive? Imagine taking on the high cost of energy with the gusto of attacking Wal-Mart and really helping the voting public a little instead of filling the coffers to pay for the next election. How about term limits to prevent any office holder from becoming so powerful as to overrule any attempt to challenge him? These ideas will happen when the electorate decides to take control of the power given to them in the vote and start to vote values instead of the easy way out. When concern replaces apathy, we may have a chance to get our government back in the form that the founders meant for us to have.

Liberals and Conservatives

The spectrum of political philosophy has been reduced in our time to liberal or conservative, but the real spectrum needs to be brought back to light. As the spectrum of visible light that goes from the invisible infra-red long wave to the ultra-violet shorter wave, the philosophy of government is also spread from no government to complete government control. You might say that this is invisible government to the invisible individual. We have given names to the various areas as we travel this spectrum, starting with anarchy, or the lack of government, on the right to the brutal totalitarian dictatorship on the left. The mid sections are where we usually argue about liberalism and conservatism, but many do not understand that much of our argument is about other forms of government rather than the interpretation of the Constitution.

The Constitutional form of government was an experiment that placed a society in the middle of the two opposing ends of the governmental spectrum, with enough government to protect our society and aid in its commerce but still allow individual freedoms to exist. Interpretation of the Constitution is usually reduced to examining the intent of the founding fathers. Depending upon the wishes of those examiners, a broad or narrow view may be accepted. The broad interpretation (or the liberal thought) is not the opposite of the narrower (or conservative thought) as presented by our politicians, but just a small difference in view of the original meaning. If one were to go beyond this type of interpretation, a different form of government would have to be considered. An example of a liberal interpretation would be that the airspace over a state is controlled by the federal government for the purpose of air transportation. I am sure that the founders did not think about airplanes flying across the country and having to control their traffic patterns. The states had to give up their rights of controlling their airspace, and we have a liberal view that has worked. The conservative view would have been to maintain the states' rights over the airspace above them.

Other changes in our way of government through the legislative process have gone beyond the conservative or liberal interpretation and entered into drastic changes to the Constitution. The graduated income tax flies in the face of the Constitutional idea of equal treatment under the law. To tax me at a greater rate than my neighbor because I work more hours and make more money than he does is not the wish of our founders and was not a liberal or conservative problem. Redistribution of wealth is not in our Constitution and is the property of Communism. By adding this to our system of government, we lost some of our freedom to work and compete equally with each other and the rest of the world. The cry that it is unfair for the poor to have to pay taxes at the same rate has nothing to do with the way in which our Constitution was written, and there are many ways in which to help the poor without stifling the wages of the people that create the jobs for everyone. We are still arguing this question and probably have to assume that is part of the way we live now, but the loss of freedom was great, and very few Americans realize that we have incorporated a little communism into our way of governing ourselves.

Another way in which we have viewed liberalism in the wrong way is the incorporation of socialism into our way of government. Social Security is a socialistic program, and we see much of the legislation to provide benefits for various needs as the incorporation of socialism into our Democratic republic. The Medicare program and the welfare programs are socialism in the basic form, but most of us do not view these programs as such. These are not interpretations of the Constitution but additions of other forms of government to it without amendments. We call them the liberal agenda, but it really is the introduction of other forms of government.

Something that has always given me a little chuckle is the fact that the start of the Republican Party was at the time of the Civil War. The man at the helm was Abraham Lincoln, who was the most liberal president in the history of our country. I am sure that many will argue with me, but wait and hear this. He changed the Constitution to state that a black man was five fifths of a man rather than three fifths and changed the nation from that of a slave-owning republic to freedom for all. His interpretation of the idea that all men are created equally was true for all and not just white men. His changes to the way of life and government were as far from conservatism as one could get without total revolution, yet he is the father of the Republican Party that thinks of itself as the conservative side of the political spectrum.

The people that call themselves by the label of liberal or conservative are kidding themselves into believing that they truly belong to a political philosophy that is the best avenue for our country. As we hear these people debate constantly on the news shows and in the papers, we also see the same news media adhering to one side or the other. The real truth is that many politicians are more interested in special interest groups than constitutional interpretation. Many of the supporters of both groups are more interested in their own special projects than in following a political philosophy. Examples of this are the pro-life and pro-choice groups.

The politician that is truly interested in the care and protection of our citizens has to be both liberal and conservative to be able to react to the changing ways in which we live. The age of machines, electronics and transportation have caused us to take a second look at what the founders were trying to do, and we have to be very careful to protect the basic freedoms we enjoy as we react to the new situations presented to us each day. The use of band aids and quick fixes many times steals freedom without anyone noticing until the next problem. Recently the Supreme Court of the United States of America ruled that a local governmental body could take its citizen's property for the private use of another. I could not believe what I was hearing. We have decided that the individual that so much blood has been spilled to protect has been reduced to nothing more than expendable for the good of a contractor that will guarantee more tax dollars or jobs. All of the sudden we are all at risk and at the mercy of our local and state governments. Moral and ethical treatment of citizens has been replaced by greed and the need to get reelected. Political philosophies have been used as labels but are forgotten when not in the best interest of the politician. Special interests have taken over.

The Republican Party that touts itself as the conservative party, or the ones that are dedicated to preserve the basic freedoms and the Constitution, are really more interested in the upper ends of the economic ladder, and the larger the corpo-ration, the greater the access to their agenda. The Democratic Party, while being funded by the huge corporate interests for the same reason as the Republicans, have sold out to the athe-ists, secularists, the abortionists, the homosexual interests and the labor unions and have sent all values into the sewer. The Christian religion is called the religious right, which I think is humorous because I cannot find the religious left.

For either party to express any value system is suicide in the news media, and our educational institutions have become insti-tutes for liberalism, socialism and communism study with the expressed purpose of producing Democrats that think alike and have the same agenda. Conservatives and their ideology are not allowed on campus, and as colleges and universities protect the free speech of their leftist professors, they allow those same pro-fessors to lower grades on the students that disagree with their political thought. Lately, it has become dangerous for a conser-vative to try to lecture or speak on campus; they're met with rude behavior and a complete lack of respect for any opposing view. What a disservice our young are getting in the name of education.

When I attended Syracuse University, my advanced inor-ganic chemistry professor gave a fifteen minute speech before each class that denounced the American government and claimed it needed change. He was from England and said that we should adopt their parliamentary form of government. When I challenged him about why he was teaching in the United States instead of in England, he became furious. I knew why he was here—because his PhD. could not be traded for a title in England, and therefore he was just another person without privilege. My chemistry class was greatly compromised because of his political discourse and my tuition wasted, except for getting a degree. Learning chemistry had been a side issue.

"Conservative" and "liberal" are just names to separate politicians and try to describe their slant on the problems at hand, but many times they reverse their stripes, and the names just cover up the special interest they are really supporting.

Religion

You would expect this chapter to be about the presence of a value system rather than the absence of same, but do not be surprised if that is not the case. Religion has been the place that we have trusted to provide societies with the values of civility. The Ten Commandments and the Golden Rule have guided us in how we approach the formation of laws and statutes in our attempts to protect and preserve the rights and privileges of citizens. Of course, the framework of a structure of laws is within the allowed freedoms granted to a people by their governing body. The weekly attendance of churches, synagogues and mosques by their members has provided constant training and revisiting in the tenets of each of the Western religions. One would think that the world should be a great place with all of this effort at teaching these ancient laws and proverbs. Quite the opposite has happened.

Today our country is battling an extremist group consisting of radical Muslims that have decided that those that are not believers in their form of religion should be perished from the earth. Our way of life contrasts greatly with the religious zeal with which these adherents think life should be lived. Forcing all to believe as they do is their mission, and dying to cause great harm to others is not a problem for them. It seems outrageous to us that a people would strap bombs to their children and send them into a crowded area with women and children for the sole purpose of blowing themselves up to take the lives of many others. To twist the will of God to believe that this is somehow the way to paradise is beyond the understanding of any normal human being. Justifying the killing of innocent people by teaching that this is the true intent of their religion is to pervert one of the great religions of the world. Of course, this is not the first time this has happened.

The Golden Rule that tells us to "*Do unto others as you would have others do unto you*" has been misinterpreted for many years, going back to the start of Christianity. The Ten Commandments have been in text form for three thousand years and have been used to both build societies and justify tearing them down. We do not have to go back very far to see the perversion of religion to advance a tyrant's wishes, and if we look at the thirteenth through sixteenth centuries, we find the Holy Roman Empire using religion to purge the world of heretics by burning them at the stake. The Inquisition against nonbelievers was a full all out war against any thought to believe differently than the way the church was teaching at the time. Since very few people could read and the Bible was in Latin and Greek, the church interpreted every part as they saw it, and most of the interpreters were not educated and could read very little. The power of the church became more political than religious, and this power allowed opponents to be taken care of as heretics without question. Somehow God's wishes had been felt to some that nonbelievers should be killed in a most horrendous manner.

Later, during the protestant reformation, the killing continued with Catholics killing Protestants and Protestants killing Catholics and others they deemed nonbelievers. The Protestants used drowning more often than fire, but the results were the same. People were killed in the name of religion by the radical elements of the day. It was not much different than today, except there were fewer places to run and hide. The differences between the Catholic Church and the Church of England caused the deaths of many. Queen Mary was given the title of Bloody Mary for her acts of butchery against those clinging to the Church of England when she decided to change back to the Roman Church. The laws of Moses and the Golden Rule were the same then as now, but somehow they were perverted and reinterpreted to allow just the opposite of what they meant. The commands that basically say "thou shalt not kill" and "treat each other as you would be treated" had taken on the meaning of "only kill those that disagree with you, and do it to others before they can retaliate."

The perversion of religions did not stop then and has not stopped in our day. At the conquering of the Americas by the British, French, Spanish and Portuguese, the Christians of these countries allowed the killing of the Aztecs, Incas, American Indians, and many of the native peoples of two continents. It is estimated that about six million natives in Brazil were killed when the Europeans came as conquerors. The same number killed was during the Second World War in the Holocaust, but the Brazilians, because of their status as natives that were thought to be less than human, it is hardly mentioned in world history. Christians killing people in huge numbers was not thought to be immoral or unethical to those carrying out the deed.

Most of us are familiar with the trouble in Ireland and lately the Christians in Serbia trying to purge Yugoslavia of Muslims, but we do not seem to put these acts in the same category as the Muslim extremists we are facing today. The one glaring fact is that all of this is the corruption of man when he tries to apply religion to political problems. Religions are shaped to our liking, and it is very difficult for us to shape ourselves to the laws of the religion. The values of respect for your neighbor and demonstrating a willingness to help him or saving life instead of taking it are too often replaced with our own vices that we call religion. Can you imagine a world that adheres to the Ten Commandments? As the song says, "Wouldn't it be wonderful." After the Second World War, the Christian community realized that it was the Christians in Germany that did not oppose Hitler, and the Vatican did not condemn the Holocaust until after the war. After all of these years of history showing us the result of the zealous believer, we have not seemed to learn anything. History has repeated itself over and over again. It is still happening.

The struggle against religion in the United States and Europe may have some basis if you look at what religious fanatics have been able to do throughout the world. Freedom to practice the religion of one's choice is given in much of the world, but when that practice is offensive to others, the practice of religion can be compromised. The fact that this country was created with documents that are extensions of the Judeo-Christian ethic is in the writing, and the thought that this in itself was the establishment of a religion is somehow being put forward as a way to attack the very freedoms expressed by this ethic. The Ten Commandments on the courthouse wall is not an attempt to convert people to Judaism, but to remind us that our laws have descended from this ancient text. The right to life, liberty and the pursuit of happiness in the Declaration of Independence is not an attempt to convert anyone to a religious discipline but to explain where these rights were thought to have come from by our founders. It is amazing to me when people decide to use

God when it benefits their agenda and to deny God when it forces them into a value system they wish not to join. When we look at the opposition to religious articles in the public domain, it is taken for granted that religion is the object of opposition. In truth, the real object is the value system we have incorporated into our society.

Family values as stressed in most religions is opposite to the wishes of those that foster the idea of non-procreating families or the homosexual union. As each of us should be free to live as we please within our homes, it is not in the best interest of this or any other nation to tear down the value of the procreating family. Discarding traditional family values and trying to legislate both ends of the digestive system into sex organs is an abomination in any society.

The big movie being pushed for an Academy Award this year is part of the homosexual agenda, and the entertainment and news media are putting this movie's preview on the air each day. There are no laws that prevent or discourage two men or two women living together, so why are we being bombarded with the idea of legislating rights to do what is already legal. The agenda of homosexual unions and living together without the benefit of marriage have become more important than the entertainment value of many movies and television shows. Many of our religious bodies have succumbed to these phenomena and accepted that which destroys the idea of true family values. Once again, man has bent the tenets of religious doctrine to favor that which he wishes instead of obeying that which is taught in his religious texts.

The other day I was sitting at the counter of a local restaurant having a bowl of their famous chili when another patron asked someone what was being built across the road. He was told that it was a church. After hearing the response, the patron said that there must be a lot of money in religion. The church being built may be the largest in our area and is costing millions of dollars. This is the second building this congregation has built in a very short time because of their tremendous growth. As this church is being built, others are being abandoned, and the transfer from church to church goes on as people try to find an answer to their spiritual questions.

My church has lost more than ten percent of its members in the last few years to other churches of the same denomination, but the planning committee has decided that we should remodel the choir loft and replace the electronic sound system because some think it would enhance the sound of the choir. As we have not been able to raise enough money to meet the budget and pay apportionments to the conference, I voted against this project, but it is moving ahead. The idea that we should be entertained and feel good while in church for one hour each week is not from a passage in the Christian Bible but seems to be in the hearts of those that claim to be believers. Taking care of ourselves instead of others has become the main purpose of raising money. I suggested that the monies raised for this project be given to Katrina victims to repair or build new churches. The suggestion was not considered or brought to a vote. Apparently helping someone else before helping ourselves is out of the question.

The great religions of the world that claim to want peace and respect for each individual have failed us, with the values they teach being twisted into self indulgence and hatred of others. It is no secret that more people have been killed in the name of religion than any other cause, and we still cannot learn anything as we try to apply our respective religious faiths to our way of life. Confessing and praying on the Sabbath and then running the nearest stoplight as you leave to go home is the norm. Christmas time each year is wonderful because people actually smile at each other and try to be a little more civil in their relationships. We find that, because some believe that the word "Christmas" is religious, even this time of peace and understanding should be stopped and substituted with the word "holiday," which would make it just another Memorial Day or Labor Day. You do not have to be religious to celebrate Jesus Christ's birthday since there is historical evidence of his birth and existence. We celebrate the birthdays of other famous people without the idea that we will believe everything that they said or did. The idea that religion will taint those that do not believe if it is in the public space is personal and not constitutional.

Religions and their basic teachings may be the last place that we as civilized societies have a chance to maintain and enhance a system of values. The failure of our churches, synagogues and mosques to be represented by the true values given for their existence has reduced our value system as much as the erosion caused by those that do not subscribe to a religious belief.

Lawyers

You probably thought that lawyers were going to escape my scrutiny, but it would be difficult to discuss values and not include the keepers of our legal system. The Bar is the professional group that is responsible for the formation of our country. John Adams as a lawyer used his legal training to argue for independence and later to write the Massachusetts Constitution, which became the guideline for the United States Constitution. Today we see lawyers advertising for business by asking us to find someone to sue. They will get money for us if we do, and we should not try to settle any claim without their help. But the need for the legal profession is great and will continue as our legal system becomes more complex.

Most laws expressed by a language are open to interpretation because the language is not precise enough or leaves other questions unanswered. For an example, let us go to the sixth commandment of *Do not kill.* After writing this into law, you would assume that killing was a crime, but when a police officer kills to defend himself, is that the same crime? Next, the need for using deadly force by a police officer has to be explained; and after that, what does deadly force consist of? One law requires many more to define its true meaning, with some never defined properly and then the courts have to make the judgment. As you can see, the need for legally trained professionals is essential for both the making of laws and then interpreting them when in use.

Most state houses of government and the Congress are made

up of representatives that have been trained in the legal profession. The good part of this is the fact that laws are passed that usually meet the requirements of the respective Constitutions and the United States Constitution. The bad part is that many bills are passed that favor the legal profession and increase the litigiousness of our society.

Recently, the State of West Virginia passed a bill revoking the use of third party liability in suits to establish cause and damages in accidental injuries. Since I am not a lawyer, I do not understand all of the ramifications but do know that the auto insurance industry was greatly in favor of this bill passing. My auto insurance agent told me that if I were to have an accident that involved another car and someone was riding in my car, both myself and my passenger could be sued for damages or my insurance company may have to pay double. Of course this doubled the fees that the lawyers would receive, and they fought against the bill with hubris. When the bill passed, our insurance rates were supposed to decline because of the reduction of the legal fees paid by the insurance companies, as they defended their clients twice for each accident. While the lawyers argued that the bill would destroy the method of keeping insurance companies honest, it really seems to have been only a vehicle to enrich the lawyers. Apparently there was a law on the books that had a main purpose of helping lawyers.

The same case was made for the medical doctor's malpractice insurance. We were losing doctors in our state because they could not afford the insurance needed to protect their liability in medical matters. The law was changed by capping damage amounts but fought bitterly by the trial lawyers to protect the pot of gold they had been tapping for some time.

Many times we see laws passed that are for special inter-ests, and if the legislature is made up of lawyers, it is natural that their inspired legislation would benefit them. I have won-dered if the quest for litigation has been in the back of legisla-tors' minds when they appropriate money for traffic control or half-heartedly reduce police forces for budgetary reasons instead of increasing them for crime fighting. Many of the suits and tri-als present today could be avoided with proper legislation and enforcement of the laws presently on the books, but this never seems to be the direction of government. It has always bothered me that someone that had sworn to uphold the laws of the land spent so much time trying to circumvent those same laws for political or financial reasons.

The area of law that affects all of us is the area of litigation. Eventually all of us have to pay the damages awarded, and as with sports, the costs are hidden from view. Many years ago, a friend of mine related to me his experience as a juror on a case against the local power company. It seems that a local trailer park had a rule that prevented the installation of television antennas on the roofs of trailers. One resident disobeyed this rule and was installing an antenna on his trailer when he accidentally pushed it into the electrical wires over head. The result was his death by electrocution. His widow had retained a lawyer and was suing the power company for complacency in the death of her husband. My friend told me that the power company proved that their wires were at the legally prescribed height and were within all guidelines and statutes. He said that after holding up the jury's verdict against the power company for a whole day, he gave in to the pressure. The widow against the large company was too much for the jury, and so what if the power company did nothing wrong? It would not hurt them to help out this poor woman. The power company was actually quite small, and our rates went up the next year. Emotion and psychology won the case, with the law being an afterthought.

Using emotion to gain huge settlements is one of the ways in which the legal system makes a lot of money. Another example is in the trial of criminals where the criminal is made to look as if they were the victim and vice versa. One case of a felony charge against a person that I knew involved the charge that he had destroyed property belonging to his former girlfriend. I was given a subpoena to testify as a character witness on his behalf, and as I entered the court room, I noticed that the former girl-friend was in a wheelchair. Later I learned that she had a disease that she had contracted after the alleged incident, but the wheel-chair made it impossible for any number of character witnesses to help. The man against the girl in the wheelchair was what the jury saw, and that was what they used to reach their verdict. We saw the same thing in the OJ trial with a black jury saving a black man from the white man's justice. There was no other reason for the verdict than bias for the defendant and against the prosecution. The law had very little to do with the results of the trial. Trial lawyers are good actors, and how they portray their clients has more to do with the verdict than the facts of the case. Of course the media's attempt for ratings by trying the cases in the evening news does not help the jury in their attempt to be unbiased in the judgment used to reach a verdict.

One of the greatest misuses of the public by the legal profes-sion is the request for and the granting of huge damage rewards for liabilities against another party. The party suing could be any-one from one person to the federal government. As the discussion about the cost of medical malpractice insurance was going on, the cost of the insurance that was passed on to the patient was also discussed. It became clear that when a large settlement was granted, the action against the doctor was also against everyone that would need medical attention in the future. I was being sued every time a malpractice went to court. The awards were far and away greater than any doctor could afford, with the reason being that the patient hurt deserved it.

Would it not be great if all of us could get what we deserved every time we needed it or could prove the need? We see the same proposition put forth as the labor unions try to seek increases due to what the worker deserves rather than what the skill level to do the job is worth. The "deserve" angle permeates our society and is accepted in many areas, including the courthouse when someone has been perceived to have been hurt. The widow deserved the award, and the power company could afford it, so why not give it to her when in reality all of the power company's customers were the ones being sued? The auto company passes the cost of law suits on to their customer as do all companies that rely on customers for their income. So when a large or small company is sued, the public is the one that will foot the bill for any awards. If you do not think that the penalties and class actions against EXXON over the oil spill in Alaska had anything to do with the cost of gasoline, then you are very naive. Instead of suing the customer, I think it would be more advantageous to put the individuals that were responsible for the accident or liability on trial and sue them or put them in jail. You and I would not have to pay for their mistakes, but then the members of the Bar would lose a lot of money, and they rely on the American public to fund their activities.

During the seventies and eighties, the small airplane industry came under the ax of the of the trial lawyer. I remember reading an accident report about an airplane crash that had resulted in the death of the pilot. The pilot was the owner of a twenty-year-old airplane and had replaced the carburetor with one not recommended for that airplane engine. It malfunctioned and caused the loss of power, which resulted in the crash. The suit was against the aircraft manufacturer and the engine company, with the final reward of millions of dollars. Product liability for an airplane twenty years old that had been tampered with by an unlicensed mechanic was now the norm. The result of the product liability suits against small airplanes eventually raised the cost of these units so high that they could not be sold, and they went out of production. The airplanes used for training and transportation of individuals were no longer available to the public and had to be purchased abroad. I had heard that the product liability cost per new airplane was in the neighborhood of one hundred thousand dollars, but the airplane without this expense sold for about half that amount. For years, lawyers were suing the public and all of the pilots and future pilots to get large awards for their clients and themselves. We are still paying for the damages rewarded twenty and thirty years ago, and the idea of a deserving plaintive is still more compelling to juries than common sense and justice for the rest of the public that ends up footing the bill.

What does this have to do with values? The young lawyer accepts his license to practice law with the same type of oath as the doctor to do no harm, but the morality of the legal profession disappears when money is on the table. Years ago, I went through a divorce, and as this process started, I retained the same lawyer that I had used to complete the deed for my house. He told me that he did not usually do divorces but would for me to keep his hand in that form of practice. As we proceeded to finish the property settlement and the paperwork for the court, he would give me options of the various ways in which I could apply for and receive the decree. He would say that legally you can do this, but morally you should do it this way. Both options for each question were put on the table, and it was something that I had never heard of from a lawyer. His moral code of ethics was working, and he was not afraid to pass it on to his clients. It was never presented as a religious argument, and to this day I do not know whether or not he is religious, but I do know that he is morally sound. He is still my lawyer for anything in the legal area that comes up, and he has also become a good friend. His honesty and doing no harm is extended to both parties in any situation he is working on, and I only hope and pray there are many other lawyers like him. He proved to me that it was possible to be honest and subscribe to a value system while being successful in the legal profession. Values did not have to be thrown away to make money and deliver justice. Others did not have to pay for my awards or transgressions to satisfy a claim, so why cannot the rest of the world practice law in this manner?

Conclusion

Can We Bring Our Values Back

The idea that a value system is part of society has been the difference between civilized and non-civilized groups of humans since the beginning of time. The richness of values in civilization has steadily let us progress from the cave man to the sophisticated types of governments and freedoms that we enjoy in the twenty-first century. The idealism during the American Revolution and writing of the United States Constitution has been steadily eroded. Over time, that idealism has been replaced by the realism of the moment without regard for the future. How we try to go forward and not allow that erosion to continue to become the new revolution is an endeavor that I believe to be in our best interests. At the beginning of this book, I wrote that growing up and maturing was young idealism turning into the adult realism of accepting responsibility. That same maturation process has happened to our country, with responsibility and hard work causing us to try to invent short cuts and the easy way out. This usually causes the erosion of values that tell us to be responsible and honest with ourselves and others.

The political arena is a place that sets the tone of ethical behavior for any society, and how the governing group acts usually tells the world what the country is about. We see the Palestinians electing a terrorist group as the leaders of their attempt to become a nation rather than employ a value system that would guarantee their success. They have voted for belligerence rather than trying to be a neighbor, which will prevent them from any success in standing alone. Our own politicians have decided to argue and carry on the campaign for reelection after the election. Last evening, the president gave his State of the Union address and was followed by the opposing party's message. I have never found that an opposing message was asked for in the Constitution as the State of the Union message is. The idea that a political winner has to refight the campaign each and every day of his term is the most unproductive behavior a government body can participate in. We have polls every day that attempt to reelect or turn down our office holders by popular demand instead of letting them fulfill their terms of office. Roadblocks of constant divisiveness prevent any useful dialog to happen, and we the people are left with nothing but bickering and name-calling while the problems keep piling up and special interests run the country.

Changing the behavior of our electorate is the responsibility of the voter, and it is about time that we left the special interest causes and demand our representatives start to represent us. Voting is the most powerful weapon we have and can be made to be felt when the office holder is turned out to pasture. We have to start to take our government back and require those elected to represent us instead of the lobbyists. Revising campaign laws to allow only registered voters to contribute to reelection campaigns is an idea that would take the special interest out of the picture. The right of free speech given to individuals but also interpreted as being a right of a corporation should be reviewed. Corporate free speech allows thousands to gang up on a few. Realizing that the most important items on the politician's agenda are power, pay raises and retirement that exceeds any in the private sector should make us look a little closer at the people that we are putting into office. As we support people that tell us that they are of a particular political philosophy, we find out later that they have masked their true philosophy. Socialists and communists tell us that they are Democrats and Libertarians, and anarchists tell us they are Republicans. Each party has to be honest with us before they can expect our support, and the people they put forth to run on their tickets should represent the philosophy of that party. We cannot wait for the politician to reform because that will not happen. The idealism of those that wrote the Federalist Papers has disappeared and seems out of reach now, but with a little prod from the voters, we may see some of that idealism return.

The power of corporate America has overshadowed much of the economic issues for the individual, and government has chosen to represent that power more often than the individual. Most of the tax loopholes have been created for the corporate world and favors those that seem to have the biggest influence in Washington. The oil companies have had tax incentives for exploration of energy sources for years, yet we are still more dependent on foreign oil than ever before. The incentives have benefited profits rather than oil exploration. We see farm and crop subsidies that are given mainly to corporate agricultural companies but do not help the individual farmer competing with the whole world for a market for his grain. Corporate involvement in government is sometimes proportional to the amount of money available as campaign and lobbying funds. We see huge drug companies winning out over the smaller generic companies on patent issues and other regulatory issues. The complete Senate being persuaded to favor a foreign company over United

States companies is the result of lobbying and money being more important than being representatives of their constituents.

The great wealth of these multinational corporations puts them in the forefront, and their message is heard before any others. But as non-human entities, they should be last. While it is important for corporate America to be recognized by government for economy maintenance and growth, it is also necessary for these same corporations to become the same good citizens as is expected of each individual. We are being told that the economy is very good now, but the fast food employee has been forced to work two to four more hours a week to buy gasoline to get to work. The economy is worse this year than last year for him and thousands like him. His contribution to the greed of multinational corporations is keeping him poor.

When the corporate executive leaves his religion, honesty, integrity and the welfare of his neighbor at the door before entering to go to work, we have to remind him or her that they have become just another common criminal as is happening in the Enron case as well as the other cases that have come to trial. The idea that values become unnecessary as we hide behind the corporate veil has to stop, and we need to trust the operators of our economic success to have the same value system as we use in our daily lives.

How would you like to have your illnesses treated out of compassion rather than for money? Sounds great, but hoping for cheap, compassionate care for medical problems is like hoping to win every lottery in the country on the same day. A medical community that charges the poorest people the highest rate because they cannot afford insurance is unconscionable and has to be changed. A system of applying medical aid to a society that allows constant abuse of the taxpayer and patient is far from my idea of a free enterprise system. It is a system full of fraud, theft and misuse of each of us in this country. To only treat the wealthy with the best available and the poor with what is left may be true freedom from government control, but we have a great amount of government control, and it still is the way the system works. Making money off of the illness and misfortune of others is abhorrent to me, and yet our government sponsors this very thing when they allow elements outside of the medical field to profit from Medicare and insurance. We find nursing homes and hospitals running up the tab with unnecessary tests and therapies to enrich their bottom line. The compassion in medicine has turned to greed, and we have to become engaged in the system to return some of the values of honesty, integrity and respect to the practice of this most noble science. Being treated for an illness may not be a Constitutional right, but it should be more than a wish in a country that prides itself on freedom and compassion.

The entertainment, sports and news media together enter our lives constantly, and as they try to persuade us that they are compassionate and unbiased, we see the liberal slant to all that they do. Hollywood tells us to be tolerant of people of all ethnic and cultural groups but also demonstrates that *pretty, handsome* and *thin* is acceptable while *chubby* and *fat* are diseases and *homely* is curable with surgery. Looking good and having a good time is all that counts. As the media fights for gun control and abortion, they teach our kids that guns and sex organs are play things without a care for any type of value system. "Values are archaic," and "religion should be banned" are the messages taught by their actions and words every time we turn on our television sets. Perhaps it is time that we stop turning the television on and stop going to movies that are valueless. Maybe it is time to tell our cable operators that we want rates that reflect usage and not how much money was promised to a sports league. We are the consumers and have the power to change the things that offend us with our determination and quest for good and evil to be portrayed as they really are. The criminal is not the good guy, and the victim should not become a victim all over again to satisfy a television audience.

The job at the local grocery store of bagging groceries is still a minimum wage job, and the kid doing it is still paying tribute to a union for the privilege of having the job. After the twenty years since my son had the job, the union has done nothing to return something for all of the dues paid. The airline workers have lost most of their retirement, and nothing has been learned. It is time that labor unions be treated as the huge corporations that they have become just as other corporations are treated. The Sherman Anti-trust Act should be applied where needed and the greed and misconduct of the unions should be subject to the same investigations as other corporations. The main interest of the union has to return to the worker instead of political power. To take a minimum wage worker's money and give it to a political party that the worker does not back is criminal in any other private setting. All sitting Democrats should go to their local grocery store and thank the bag persons for their help and contributions. Maybe they would start to get the picture of what they are really upholding in their quest to keep union money flowing. It is time that union members demand their officers start working for better conditions as well as equal pay for both sexes and safety at the work place; and it is time they work with companies to expand job security instead of blackmailing them into bankruptcy.

Doctor Martin Luther King's wife is lying in state, and the end of one of the most important eras in American history has ended. Doctor King asked us to judge a man by his character instead of the color of his skin. Much of his work has produced results, but the problem of race is still with us and may never become extinct. As long as man is competitive, he will abase others to stay on top, and the fight for equality will never end. Those dedicated to the eradication of racial bias have taken another road that has traded the individual for political power. The NAACP and the Urban League have ignored any improvement in the black community when it does not fit with their political ideology. There is presently a black man and a black woman who are qualified for and probably could get nominated for the highest elected position in our country. Colin Powell and Condi Rice are two of the finest ambassadors this country has ever had, and both have something in common by not being role models for the black community. Rather, the role models are a mayor and city councilman who is upset that he was not considered a friend by the men that robbed him and the gangsters that pillage the inner city communities with impunity. Black community groups that spend more time accusing the police forces of bias rather than inviting them into their communities to establish law and order have forgotten the wish of Doctor King to look for character. When these things are reversed and clothing and speech emulates the Powells and Rices rather than the gangsters, maybe we can start making more headway. Forget politics, and try to inject education and a set of values into the inner city instead of protecting eugenics and pants worn with the crotches at the knees. Start building the character that many of us have started to look for, and you will be amazed at your success.

I have always been taught that a good education did not teach one what to think, but how to think. Our education system has steadily declined in quality for many years, and the idea of trying to make everything easier for our children than we experienced has backfired. Teacher unions have addressed work hours, wages and qualification instead of teaching quality and student reactions. We see teachers striking with the lesson to their students that if something is not what you want just stop until you get your way. The world does not work that way, and the student that does not learn how to compete will not achieve his share of the wealth. My sister-in-law tells me that parents are requesting that their sons and daughters be moved to classes below the college entrance level because the homework is too hard for them. Parents are telling their children to fail before they have had a chance at life.

Universities that used to offer a liberal arts and science education now offer an education to teach students how to be liberals. Narrow-mindedness has replaced the open mind that is taught to soak in all ideas and learn to process them into their rightful areas. Becoming educated was becoming the person with the ability to think for oneself, but today the university teaches political theory in all classes. I was taught to dislike the American form of government in an advanced chemistry class, and my niece was told that being conservative was not the way to get good grades in English class. Higher education has exploded into ideology workshops, and many students are left with only high payments of college loans and nothing to help them compete in the world. We need to stop supporting those institutions that discriminate against political beliefs as they repel those that discriminate against sexual preferences. My alma mater will not let the Boy Scouts use their facilities because of their ban on gay scout leaders but insist that only liberal political theory be taught and accepted. I have yet to meet a family that would like their son to camp with a gay scout leader, weather or not they have any other prejudice against the homosexual community, but this discrimination is the reason that scouts cannot use their facilities. What a pity for any institution to enforce their thoughts and wishes on others as they ignore the basic idea of educational values of open minds and learning to think for ourselves. To narrow education to one side of the political spectrum is only half of an education, and that is what we are getting today from many of the most prestigious institutions.

Education takes a long time to fix, and if we start now it will take another generation for the effect to be seen. We had better start soon, or another generation will be thrown away. A good start would be for universities to upgrade their education curricula for the teachers they are graduating since the teaching agenda is now at the bottom of the educational ladder. Poor students end up as poor teachers, and this has to stop.

Religion is not very popular today in the media, and the secularist is constantly at work to remove any vestiges of it from society. Since religions in all forms have been the carrier of value systems, it is important that we as a nation recognize that fact and accept religion in the public areas as reminder of the need for value systems. You do not have to believe in a religion to benefit from the values taught by that religion. Being reminded to respect your neighbor is not religious but is necessary if you plan to live next door. The members of the great religions have to remind themselves of the responsibility to adhere to the tenets of their respective religions and not to manmade laws that have perverted the original intent. Working with snakes and total immersion do not a Christian make, and strapping an explosive belt on your children was not what Mohammed preached. It is so important that the values of the great religions be kept in front of us, even when we disagree, to make us think before we act or teach or demonstrate. What we do as individuals is magnified into our societies and can affect the future of our children in their quest to keep our founders' dreams in front of them.

Somehow the values of honesty, respect, loyalty, truth and integrity have to be brought back into our society as the virtues needed to progress into the future.

TATE PUBLISHING & *Enterprises*

Tate Publishing is committed to excellence in the publishing industry. Our staff of highly trained professionals, including editors, graphic designers, and marketing personnel, work together to produce the very finest books available. The company reflects the philosophy established by the founders, based on Psalms 68:11,

"THE LORD GAVE THE WORD AND GREAT WAS THE COMPANY OF THOSE WHO PUBLISHED IT."

If you would like further information, please call
1.888.361.9473
or visit our website
www.tatepublishing.com

TATE PUBLISHING & *Enterprises*, LLC
127 E. Trade Center Terrace
Mustang, Oklahoma 73064 USA